A HISTORY OF

JAMES ISLAND

SLAVE DESCENDANTS & PLANTATION OWNERS

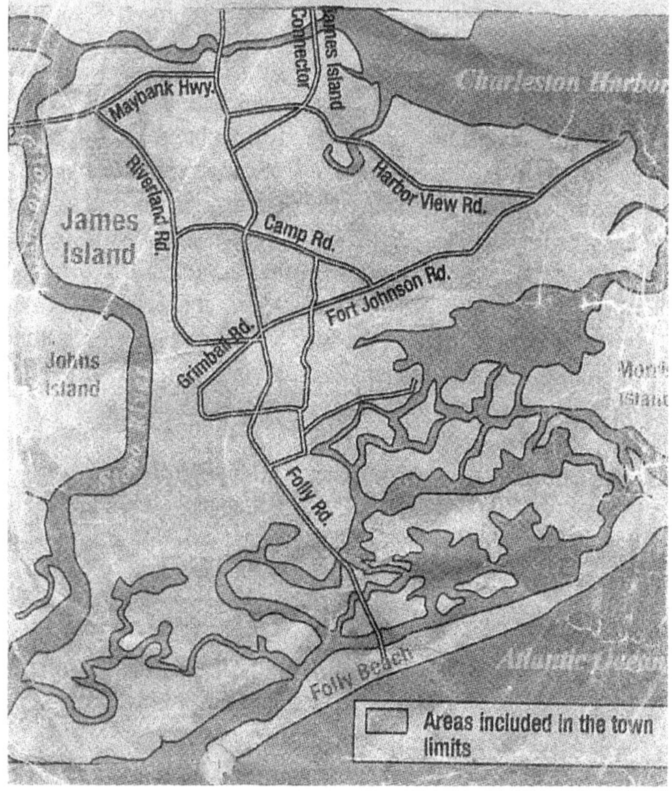

Map of James Island. *Courtesy of Charleston County Library.*

A HISTORY OF JAMES ISLAND SLAVE DESCENDANTS & PLANTATION OWNERS

the bloodline

EUGENE FRAZIER SR.

Published by The History Press
Charleston, SC 29403
www.historypress.net

First published 2010

Manufactured in the United States

ISBN 978.1.59629.976.4

Library of Congress Cataloging-in-Publication Data

Frazier, Eugene, Sr.
A history of James Island slave descendants and plantation owners : the bloodline / Eugene Frazier, Sr.
p. cm.
ISBN 978-1-59629-976-4
1. James Island (S.C.)--Genealogy. 2. African Americans--South Carolina--James Island--Genealogy. 3. Whites--South Carolina--James Island--Genealogy. 4. Slaves--South Carolina--James Island--Genealogy. 5. Plantation owners--South Carolina--James Island--Genealogy. 6. Plantations--South Carolina--James Island--History. 7. Registers of births, etc.--South Carolina--James Island. 8. James Island (S.C.)--Biography. 9. African Americans--South Carolina--James Island--Biography. 10. Whites--South Carolina--James Island--Biography. I. Title.
F277.B3F725 2010
975.7'915--dc22
2010013960

Notice: The information in this book is true and complete to the best of our knowledge. It is offered without guarantee on the part of the author or The History Press. The author and The History Press disclaim all liability in connection with the use of this book.

This book is dedicated to my wife, Francis; our son, Eugene, and his wife, Lee Frazier; my daughters, Angela D. Jenkins and Geraldine Frazier Minter, and Geraldine's husband, Byron Minter; my grandchildren, Eugene III, Gregory, Jamal, Leah, Jehrica and Brian; my great-granddaughter, Kaylee; and the descendants of both slaves and slave owners who supported me during the researching, compiling and writing of this book. I am deeply grateful for all of their support. Also, special thanks to my granddaughter Jehrica for her extra help and expertise.

Contents

PREFACE

This book was written for anyone who is interested in the history of James Island. It chronicles the genealogy of slaves and their stories, along with their pictures and the pictures of numerous plantation owners, following the slavery, sharecropping and farming era on James Island during the period from 1732 through the 1970s.

While doing my research, I relied heavily on information obtained from the U.S. Census Bureau, interviews of family members and other supporting documentation in an effort to determine the exact age of the individuals included in this book. There were some instances where ages were ascertained by family members through deductions and guesses, as many slaves did not read and write and, as a result, did not leave any written documentation. Therefore, family members often relied on oral history in regard to age and birth dates. In addition to census reports and interviews, I also investigated other sources, including records from different courts, to obtain the most accurate information possible. Thus, research results and conclusions expressed are mine and have not been endorsed by the U.S. Census Bureau.

Conversations and interviews were held over the years with descendants of slaves and descendants of slave owners. During these interviews, I was referred to by the following names: Gene, Son, Eugene, Frazier and Detective.

INTRODUCTION

James Island

James Island is located approximately seven miles west of downtown Charleston. It is surrounded by the Wappoo Creek, the Stono River and the Atlantic Ocean. In 1899, a one-lane wooden bridge was built across the Wappoo Creek, connecting the island to the peninsula at Charleston. Prior to 1899, the only access to and from James Island was by ferry or boat.

James Island is rich with African American heritage and culture. Ever since the 1700s, when blacks were first brought to James Island, the environment resembled more of a village where people depended and relied on one another. This type of environment existed until well into the 1960s. During and following the slavery and farming eras, James Island was known for the planting and harvesting of rice, cotton, tomatoes, Irish and sweet potatoes, string beans, corn, cucumbers, cabbage, okra, collard greens, eggplants and many other types of vegetables. The vegetables were sold nationally, internationally and locally at the Charleston Market on Meeting Street or at various roadside stands dotting the Lowcountry. Many of the plantations also raised livestock and poultry such as turkey, chicken, geese and duck.

Due to the unbearable hardship of slavery, sharecropping and farming on James Island, many former slaves and their descendants migrated north to escape the degradation of their living conditions. Many of them would choose never to return. However, their roots, their memories and their influence remain.

This one-lane wooden bridge was built across the Wappoo Creek between 1899 and 1900. It connected James Island to the city of Charleston. *Courtesy of South Carolina Historical Society.*

James Island is one of the few places in the United States where descendants of slaves can easily trace their roots to one of seventeen slave plantations. It has now developed into a modern-day community. For many African Americans, it is hard to imagine how far this small island has come. It has left them with a legacy of both the joy and the pain of living in a time and place wrought with hardship but somehow still intermingled with the happiness that comes only from a community built on family, love, strength and honor. It is a legacy that is impossible to forget.

This book contains the names, pictures, stories and histories of various James Island families and their bloodlines, beginning with slavery and continuing into the 1970s. It also contains pictures and information on some of the plantation owners and their descendants. In addition, this book pays homage to our men and women of the United States military and African American pioneers from James Island and surrounding areas. The majority of the images in this book have never been printed or released before.

McLeod Plantation

Owners

William "Willie" McLeod was born in 1885. He was the son of William W. McLeod, who was born in 1850, and Hallie McLeod, who was born in 1849. He was the grandson of William Wallace (1820) and Susan McLeod (1822).

Mr. Willie, as he was called, was the last owner and farmer of the McLeod Plantation. He died in 1995 at the age of one hundred. He was never married and had no children. He left his estate to the Historic Society of Charleston. During the Civil War, the Confederate army and the Union's black Fifty-fourth Regiment from Massachusetts occupied the property. The McLeod House, which was also known as the "Big House," was used as a hospital for wounded soldiers during the war.

During the early 1940s, I helped my mother and sisters harvest peanuts on the McLeod farm. After Mr. McLeod harvested his peanuts, he would turn the field over to the black people on the island. This particular field was located on the south side of Folly Road near the James Island Shopping Center, at the intersection of Folly Road and Maybank Highway. Arby's Restaurant now occupies this area.

The slave cabins on the McLeod Plantation were built in the 1850s. Six of these cabins still exist today. At the end of the Civil War, the government set up what became known as the Freedmen's Bureau. The head of each slave family in the Sea Island area was to be given land,

and as a result, some of the families on James Island were given acreage following slavery. There were many descendants of slaves who lived in the McLeod cabins through the 1970s. The McLeod Plantation is the only one of the seventeen plantations on James Island left intact.

Left: William "Willie" McLeod. *Courtesy Friends of McLeod.*

Below: Slave cabins at the McLeod Plantation. *Family picture.*

Slaves and Their Descendants

Steve and Eva Forest

Steve Forest and his wife, Eva.
Courtesy of Steven Forest.

Steve Forest was born in 1906, and his wife, Eva, was born in1912. Steve was the son of Stephen Forest Jr. (1870) and the grandson of slaves Stephen Sr. (1844) and Harriet Forest (1844). Eva was the daughter of Harry (1875) and Lavinia Green (1890).

At the outbreak of the Civil War, Brigadier General S.R. Gist of the Confederate army issued an order to evacuate James Island. Each plantation owner was allowed to leave one male and one female slave behind to watch over his plantation during the war. William Wallace McLeod entrusted his property to his slaves Stephen Sr. and wife Harriet Forest.

During the 1920s through the 1950s, Steve, the grandson of Stephen, worked at Welch's Service Station as a station attendant. His duties included changing oil, pumping gas, changing spark plugs and making minor repairs on car engines. He also drove the station's tow truck when needed. The station was located at the intersection of the old Folly Road and Maybank Highway on the McLeod Plantation. During this time, it was the only service station on the island. Steve and his family lived in one of the McLeod slave cabins until the 1950s. It still stands on the plantation as of this writing.

During a conversation with Lois R. Fields, granddaughter of Steve and Eva, she said:

> *Frazier, my grandmother taught me how to love my family and to care for people. I spent weekends with her and on Sunday she would make sure I went to Sunday school and church. She told me many stories about my great-grandfather and prepared me for the things that I would encounter in the world today. She was a religious person who believed in God, and loved all of her grand's dearly.*

Many descendants of Steve and Eva Forest still live on James Island.

Emma Line Dawson

Emma Line Dawson was born in 1863. She was married to Stephney Dawson, who was born in 1862. Stephney was the son of slaves, William (1840) and Charity Dawson (1841), and the grandson of Pompey (1821) and Judy Dawson (1835), slaves on the McLeod Plantation.

Pompey was known by his nickname "Hardtime." While he worked in the fields, he would often sing and chant that old Negro song, "Motherless Chillins see a Hardtime." This, according to his descendants and the descendants of other former slaves, was the reason he got his nickname. Pompey was on the list of slaves who were given land by the Freedmen's Bureau. However, during the late 1880s, the land was taken from him and returned to the McLeod Plantation owner.

Emma Line Dawson. *Courtesy of Deloris Dawson.*

During conversations with Deloris Dawson, the granddaughter of Emma Line and Stephney, Deloris said:

> *Frazier, I grow up living with my grandmother and grandfather. We use to talk about planting vegetables when I was very young, pick beans, sweet potatoes, how to hoe the grass from around the vegetables when it grows around them; how to break the corns off the stock, how to shell the lima beans and peas. She would always encourage me to go to Sunday school and church. She was a religious woman and this was one of the reason I joined Bethel Church when I was eleven years old. I am still a member of Greater Bethel Church on Central Park Road. Frazier, she was a short, sweet lady with long salt and pepper black hair.*

She continued:

> *Grandfather Stephney never talked as much as grandmother. He was always busy plowing the field with his mule and working on the farm. He was kind and always gave me a nickel and dime. Time was hard during those years and we could buy many things for a dime.*

Many descendants of Pompey and Judy Dawson still live in the Cut Bridge section of James Island.

Christopher "Jack" Delaney

Christopher "Jack" Delaney was born in 1911 and was married to Carrie Bell Delaney. Jack was the son of Joseph Sr. (1884) and Catharine Delaney (1892) and the grandson of Solomon "Saul" Jr. (1870) and Jane Delaney (1876). He was also the great-grandson of Solomon "Saul" Sr. (1843) and Sallie Delaney (1845) and the great-great-grandson of Amelia Smith (1800). Saul Delaney (1843) was one of the former slaves given land by the government following the war.

Saul Sr. and his wife, Sallie, were slaves on the McLeod Plantation. After slavery ended, they moved to the Dill Plantation and became farmers there. He was also listed among the founding fathers of Payne RMUE Church on Camp Road and helped to build the first church organized in 1875 under the leadership of Reverend Prince "Pappy" White (1830). Saul Sr. was also one of the church's Sunday school teachers. Saul Sr.; his

Christopher "Jack" Delaney. *Courtesy of Sarah Delaney Davis.*

Ellsworth Heyward and his wife, Madelyn. *Courtesy of Bernard "Haggy" Heyward.*

son, Saul, Jr. (1870); and his mother, Amelia Smith (1800), are buried at the Dill slave cemetery on Riverland Drive. Many descendants of Saul and Sallie still live on James Island.

During my conversations with Sarah Delaney Davis, the daughter of Jack, she said:

> *Frazier, my father was a hardworking man. He worked at the Concrete Product Company in Charleston for some time. He also worked at the Charleston Naval Shipyard for a period of time and at the Murray Lasaine Elementary School on James Island as a janitor. His last job would be at the James Island Sanitation Department until his retirement. Jack was a member of Payne RMUE Church on Camp Road. He was also one of the original fifty-six men that helped organize the Sons of Elijah Masonic Lodge #457, on James Island in 1955.*

Ellsworth Heyward

Ellsworth Heyward was born in 1909. His wife, Madelyn, was born in 1910. Ellsworth was the son of John (1885) and Elouise Heyward (1887) and the grandson of slaves, Prince (1846) and Julia Heyward (1846).

Ellsworth was the first African American mortician from James Island to become a funeral director for Fielding Home for Funerals in 1939. He retired in 1971. The Heywards were slaves on the McLeod Plantation. At the end of slavery, they moved to the Dill Plantation. Many of the Heywards' descendants still live on James Island.

Thomas Welch

Thomas Welch was born in 1891. His wife, Cecile, was born in 1897. They had three sons, Croskey (1915), Thomas C. (1918) and Robert E. Welch (1925).

During the early 1900s, the majority of the land on James Island was wooded area or farmland. The roads were all dirt roads, except Folly Road, which was a two-lane road. It was paved between the 1920s and 1930s. It ran from Charleston to Folly Beach. During this time, everyone bought gasoline, oil and spark plugs or had minor maintenance work done on their cars and trucks at Welch's Service Station, the only one on James Island.

Above, left: Thomas Welch and Charlie Scott. *Courtesy of Robert E. Welch.*

Above, right: *From left to right*: Croskeys Royal Welch (1915), Thomas C. Welch Jr. (1918) and Robert Ellis Welch (1925), the sons of Thomas Welch. *Courtesy of Robert E. Welch.*

Charlie Scott was a black man who worked for the Welches for over fifty years. During one of my conversations with Robert Welch, the son of Thomas Welch, Robert said, "Frazier, my father bought Charlie seven acres of land on Bohicket Road on Johns Island during the 1950s for him and his family." Thomas Welch was known and affectionately called "Mr. Tommy" by many African Americans on James Island during that time. Many of Thomas and Cecile's descendants and relatives still live on James Island.

Joe Heyward

Joe Heyward was born in 1844, and his wife, Caroline, was born in 1860. Joe was the son of Jim (1818) and Affy Heyward (1827). They were slaves and later sharecroppers on the McLeod Plantation.

During the farming era, Joe moved his family to the Dill Plantation, where they became farmers. Joe is listed as one of the founding fathers of Payne RMUE Church on Camp Road under the leadership of Reverend Prince "Pappy" White (1830) in 1875. Many descendants of Joe and Caroline Heyward still live on James Island.

Joe Heyward (1844) and his wife, Caroline. *Courtesy of Wilburn Gilliard.*

John Robert Gathers

John Robert Gathers was born in 1925. He was married to Evelyn Gathers. John was the son of Frank "Frankie" (1893) and his wife, Julia (1902). He was the great-grandson of Gable (1831) and Hannah Gathers (1836–1932). Gable and Hannah are buried at the Devil's Nest Cemetery on the Dill Plantation.

During one of my conversations with Robersina Gathers, the daughter of John Gathers, she said:

> *Frazier, I was born and raised on the McLeod Plantation; so were my father, grandfather and mother. I witnessed them working in the field from the time I was six years old planting all type of vegetables. When it was time, I help pick beans, tomatoes, peas, peanut, collard green, cabbage and many other types of vegetables. My family lives in the third cabin from Folly Road. They were five children in the family, four live to reach adulthood, two boys and two girls. When I was about eight years old, my mother had a baby girl. She was about one year old when she died. Her name was Julia. My father built a coffin made of board and buried her in the woods behind our cabin in between Country Club Road.*

John Robert Gathers. *Courtesy of Robersina Gathers.*

She continued:

> *I moved from the McLeod Plantation when I was in my teen to the city of Charleston. My father and mother live on the plantation until the 1970s, when he moved. Mr. Willie had promise to sell my father some land on the plantation during the 1970s, so my father went back on the plantation and did maintenance work for Mr. Willie. But, he never did sign the paper selling him the land. I started visiting Mr. Willie again during the 1970s, and he allowed me to do mission work helping the blacks that was still living on the plantation.*

Hinson/Mikell Plantation

Slaves and Their Descendants

Kit and Daphney Bright

Kit Bright was born in 1863 and died in 1902. He was married to Daphney Bright, who was born in 1872. Kit was the son of Jeremiah (1835) and Sarah Bright (1835). They were slaves, sharecroppers and farmers on the Hinson, Mikell and Lawton Plantations. During an interview with Phyllis Bright Downey, a descendant of Kit and Daphney Bright, she said, "Frazier, our grandaunt Hager White [1869] who raised me and my sister told us that Dapheny married Harry Ford from Edisto Island after the death of Kit."

She continued, "Harry Ford walked some twenty-five miles through marshes, swamps and woods from Edisto and Wadmalaw Island making his way to James Island, where he would work on the Hinson and Mikell farms." My research of the Payne RUME Church's archives revealed that Hager White (1869) was listed as one of its founding mothers. Many descendants of Kit and Dapheny still live in the Fort Johnson area of James Island.

Harrison "Harry" Ford

Harrison "Harry" Ford was born in 1861. He was married to Lucile Ford, who was born in 1863. Lucille Ford was his first wife. Harry

lived on Edisto Island during the 1870s. He made his way to James Island to the Hinson and Mikell Plantations. While working on the plantations as a sharecropper and farmer, he met and married his second wife, Dapheny Bright (1872). Many descendants of Harrison Ford still live in the metropolitan area of Charleston County.

Simeon and Isabelle Pinckney

Isabelle Pinckney was born in 1828. She was married to Simeon Pinckney, who lived from 1826 to 1921. Isabella was the daughter of a slave woman, and her father was one of the white plantation owners. As a young girl, she was given to slave owner William Wallace McLeod of the McLeod Plantation to be a companion to his young daughter, Annie McLeod.

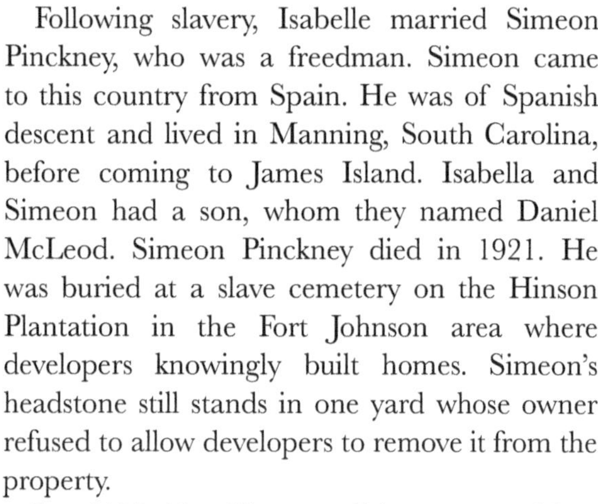

Following slavery, Isabelle married Simeon Pinckney, who was a freedman. Simeon came to this country from Spain. He was of Spanish descent and lived in Manning, South Carolina, before coming to James Island. Isabella and Simeon had a son, whom they named Daniel McLeod. Simeon Pinckney died in 1921. He was buried at a slave cemetery on the Hinson Plantation in the Fort Johnson area where developers knowingly built homes. Simeon's headstone still stands in one yard whose owner refused to allow developers to remove it from the property.

In 2009–10, Thomas Johnson, president of an organization designed to preserve and

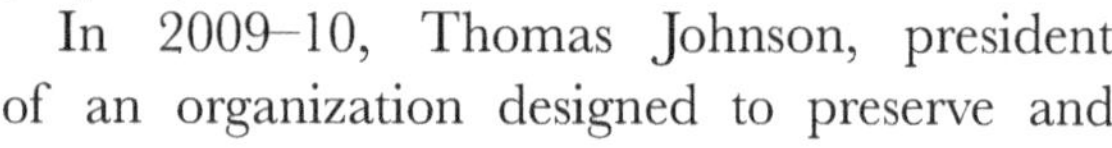

Left, top: Kit Bright. *Courtesy of Keith Bright.*

Left, middle: Daphney Bright. *Courtesy of Keith Bright.*

Left, bottom: Harrison "Harry" Ford. *Courtesy of Keith Bright.*

Above, left: Isabelle Pinckney. *Courtesy of Julius Steven Brown.*

Above, right: Headstone of Simeon Pinckney (1826–1921). *Courtesy of Julius Steven Brown.*

protect African American cemeteries on James Island, and I challenged the building of homes on identified African American cemeteries. Many builders simply ignored the laws governing cemeteries, especially those of African Americans. It has become an increasing problem, especially here in the Sea Island area and particularly in areas near rivers and creeks. Many descendants of Simeon and Isabella Pinckney still live in the Fort Johnson area of James Island.

Ephraim Ladson

Ephraim Ladson was born in 1887. His wife, Alice Ladson, was born in 1889. Ephraim was the son of slaves Fortune (1845) and Polly Ladson (1850) and the grandson of Jack (1817) and Belle Ladson (1822). The Ladsons were slaves, sharecroppers and farmers on the Hinson/Mikell Plantation.

Ephraim worked on the Hinson Plantation during the time George Nungezer farmed it. My father, Sandy Frazier, worked with Ephraim on the Hinson Plantation from the 1920s until the 1950s, when George Nungezer

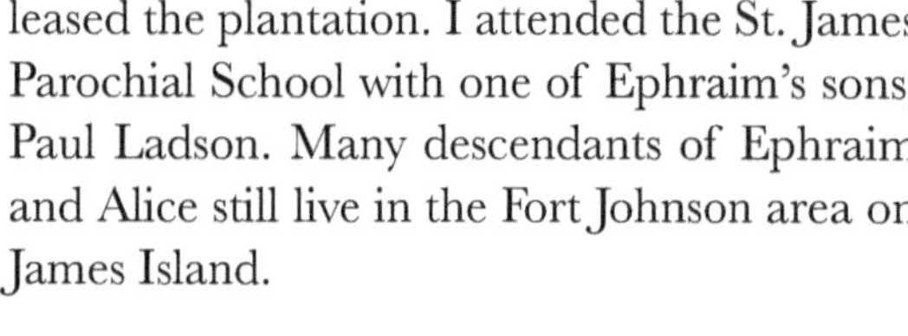

leased the plantation. I attended the St. James Parochial School with one of Ephraim's sons, Paul Ladson. Many descendants of Ephraim and Alice still live in the Fort Johnson area on James Island.

Amos and Rosa Watson

Amos Watson was born in 1902, and his wife, Rosa Watson, was born in 1905. Amos was a descendant of slaves Amos (1848) and Susan Watson (1850). Rosa was the daughter of Paul (1875) and Celia Chisolm (1876) and the granddaughter of John (1844) and Rose Chisolm (1846). Amos and Rosa worked on the Hinson Plantation during the farming era. They also had their own farm.

According to archival and oral history, Amos (1848) and Charles "Knight" Knightly (1822) were the first two former slaves registered as democratic voters on James Island in the Hunters Hall Lodge, which was later renamed Riverside Lodge Hall during the sharecropper and farming era. Many of the descendants of Amos and Rosa Watson still live on James Island.

Henry and Isabella Davis

Henry Davis was born in 1877, and his wife, Isabella Davis, was born in 1878. Henry was the son of slave John Davis (1845). Henry was born and raised on the Grimball Plantation.

Left, top: Ephraim Ladson. *Courtesy of Paul Ladson.*

Left, middle: Amos Watson. *Courtesy of Percile W. Richardson.*

Left, bottom: Rosa Watson. *Courtesy of Percile W. Richardson.*

Henry and Isabella Davis.
Courtesy of Julius Steve Brown.

As a young man, he lived and worked on the Hinson and Mikell Plantations. After he married his wife, they left Charleston and relocated to New York. According to many of his relatives, Henry and his wife returned for visits to James Island but never came back to live. However, many of Henry's and Isabella's relatives still live on James Island.

Viola "Rita" Watson Campbell

Viola "Rita" Watson Campbell was born in 1923 and died in 1961. Her husband, Joe Campbell, was born in 1922. Viola was the daughter of Amos and Rosa Chisolm Watson, the granddaughter of Paul Celia Chisolm and the great-granddaughter of John and Rose Chisolm. The Chisolms were farmers on the Grimball Plantation.

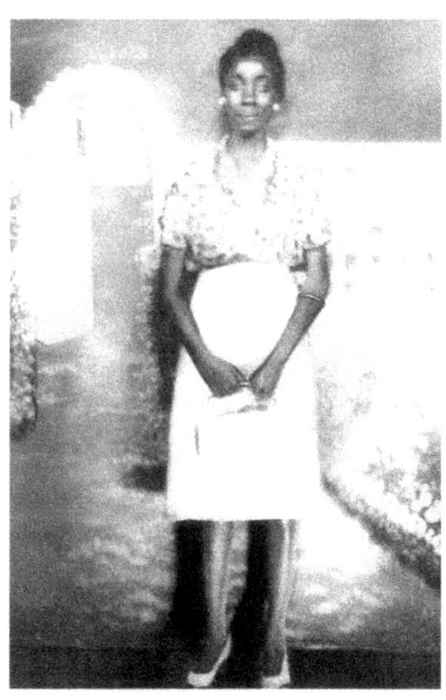

Viola "Rita" Watson Campbell. *Courtesy of Margaret W. Grippon.*

Joe was the son of Tony Campbell Jr., who was born in 1892. His wife, Celia Campbell, was born in 1898. He was the grandson of slaves, Tony Sr. (1855) and Nellie Campbell (1862), farmers on the Hinson and Seabrook Plantation. Joe and Viola were farmers on the Hinson and Mikell Plantation.

During my interview with Julia W. Mikell, Viola's sister, she said:

> *Frazier, I remember my sister as a quiet, hardworking young woman. Like many of the people in the Fort Johnson area, the only job open to blacks during that time was farm work in the field harvesting vegetables, tomatoes, corns, beans, potatoes, eggplants and many more, and some domestic work. I don't ever remember hearing my sister complaining; although, there were times when I am sure she was hurting like many others but kept it to herself. She died in 1961, in the prime of her life. I really miss her but it was "God's will" to take her home.*

Margaret W. Grippon, another sister of Viola's, said:

> *Frazier, following my sister death in 1961, at the young age of thirty-eight, she left six children behind. Three of them were too young to take care of themselves. Our mother, Rosa Watson, raised, treated and cared for them as her own. She was known and called "Rita" by the people in the community and was loving and kindhearted. She was a domestic worker, lived a quiet life and loved children. Rita became a member of St. James Presbyterian Church at an early age.*

Many of Rita and Joe Campbell's children still live on James Island.

David "Buster" and Dorothy Cromwell

David "Buster" Cromwell was married to Dorothy "Pooh" Cromwell. David was the son of David Sr. (1882) and Rose Cromwell (1892). He was affectionately called "Buster," and Dorothy was called "Pooh" by the people in the community. He worked on the Hinson Plantation when George Nungezer managed the farm. Buster was later employed by one of the local ice companies in Charleston for over twenty years until he retired. He also had a small farm of his own selling vegetables to supplement his income after his retirement.

In a letter and during my conversations with his eldest daughter, Rose, she said:

> *Frazier, our parents were poor. They worked hard to support their children. I recall how they struggled carrying wood and supplies on their shoulders from Dills Bluff to Fort Johnson Road in order to build our first house in 1956. When the family moved into our unfurnished home, we had to place newspaper inside the frame of the house. Our family did not have much,*

David and Dorothy Cromwell.
Courtesy of Dorothy Cromwell.

> *but we had each other. Everything that the children have accumulated is a result of our parents' hard work and determination to make a better life for us. We give thanks to "God" and to our parents for providing all that we have today.*

I knew David and Dorothy, and whenever I met them, they always had a kind word. They were a humble and happy couple who, like many other poor residents on the island, made the best of what they had. David and Dorothy were members of St. James Presbyterian Church. Dorothy and many of her children still live in the Fort Johnson area on James Island.

Estell "Honey" Mikell

Estell "Honey" Mikell was born in 1890. Her husband, Frank Mikell, was born in 1886. Frank was the son of slaves John (1830) and Rhina Mikell (1845) and the grandson of Warley (1797) and Joanna Mikell (1800).

During an interview with Anna Mae Fludd, granddaughter of Honey, she said:

Estell "Honey" Mikell. *Courtesy of Anna Mae Fludd.*

> *Frazier, we grew up in the Fort Johnson area of James Island. I remember my grandmother lived in a yellow wooden house in the section where we live today. The people in the community called her "Honey" and named the area where she lived "Honey Hill"; that is how Honey Hill got it name.*

She continued:

> *As a young girl, I recall my grandmother had two of every kind of animal—two cats, two pigs, two chickens and two goats. Sometimes the pigs and chickens would walk into her house like they were human. She would shoo them outside. She was the first black women in the*

Fort Johnson area and possibly on James Island to sew bed quilts and sell them in the Charleston Market and on Broad Street for fifty cent a piece. She also worked on the farm picking cotton, tomatoes, potatoes and many other vegetables. When my grandmother got too old to work on the farm, she babysat for the people in the community; she also did ironing and sewed clothes. She was also a midwife and a root doctor in the Fort Johnson area of James Island. Many people came to her house for their medicine. Although segregation was enforced in the state during those years, many white people came to Honey's house to get their medicine, and I guess that's why I never thought about segregation when I was young.

She added:

Frazier, it was a sad day when my grandmother's house burned down and she died in the fire because the fire truck was unable to get to her house because the road was not wide enough for the truck to get through. That is one of the reasons I am still fighting for the improvement in our community of Honey Hill. My grandfather, Frank "Toppy" Mikell, left James Island and lived in the city of Charleston at an earlier age.

Many descendants of the Mikells still live in the Fort Johnson area of James Island.

Joseph "Boy" and Agnes Mikell

Joseph "Boy" Mikell was born in 1906 and died in 1985. His wife, Agnes Mikell, was born in 1910. Joseph was the son of Frank (1886) and Estell "Honey" Mikell (1890) and a descendant of slaves Warley (1797) and Joanna Mikell (1800). Agnes was the daughter of James (1875) and his wife, Sarah Brown (1880).

During an interview with Anna Mae Fludd, daughter of Joseph, she said:

Frazier, my daddy was a hardworking man. His nickname was "Boy." I remember he worked for the South Carolina Highway Department and the Charleston County government paving the road from Mount Pleasant to McClellanville during the time when the roads were dirt and most of Charleston County was considered a wilderness.

Joseph "Boy" and Agnes Mikell. *Courtesy of Anna Mae Fludd.*

She continued:

Daddy would drive the truck home full of tar ready for the night shift; because, they work at night. My mother worked as a housekeeper. She raised and help educated five of us children. She loved to attend church every Sunday. She worked in our community organizing sewing clubs and did volunteer work for the American Red Cross. Records from the South Carolina Electric & Gas Company show our house was the first black family that had electricity in the Fort Johnson area of James Island.

Hattie Davis

Hattie Davis. *Courtesy of Anna Davis.*

Hattie Davis was born in 1899, and her husband, William "Bill" Davis, was born in 1888. William was the son of Fredrick (1870) and Rachel Davis (1872) and the grandson of a slave, John Davis (1845), from the Grimball Plantation.

After he came of age, William married and moved to the Lawton Plantation. The couple had six daughters, Azalea (1914), Evelina (1916), Eleanor (1917), Mary (1925), Anna (1926) and Martha (1928), and three sons, John (1929), Henry and Joseph Davis (1938).

During a conversation with Anna, she said, "Frazier, my father worked on the Lawton farm. He was a foreman during the farming time. He also had his own small farm and would work on it and sell his vegetables in the city of Charleston on Market Street." Many of Hattie's and William's descendants still live on James Island.

Dill Plantation

Owners

Pauline R. and Frances R. Dill. *Courtesy of Charleston Museum.*

Julia R. Dill was born in 1880 and died in 1970. Her sister, Pauline R. Dill, was born in 1884 and died in 1985. They also had another sister, Frances R. Dill. They were all daughters of Joseph T. (1822–1900) and Frances A. Dill (1846–1916), and the great-granddaughters of Joseph T. (1724–1796) and Sarah Dill (1742–1811).

Pauline and Frances Dill were the last descendants to own the Dill Plantation. They were never married. In their will, the Dill sisters left their plantation to the Charleston Museum to be managed as a wildlife sanctuary.

Slaves and Their Descendants

Virginia "Mama" Brown Champagne

Virginia "Mama" Brown Champagne was born in 1896 and died in 1963. She was married to Richard "Manny" Champagne, who was born in 1889 and died in 1936. Virginia was the daughter of slaves, Smiley (1845) and Grace Brown (1872), of the Dill Plantation.

Virginia and her husband were sharecroppers and farmers on the Dill Plantation during the period when Fuller King was manager of the plantation. Her house was near the Civil War Battery on the Dill Plantation, behind the area where the Food Lion Store is now located near Fort Johnson and Riverland Drive. Many of the young boys, including myself, who lived in the community played in Virginia's yard. She was affectionately called "Cousin Mama" by the children. I remember her as a quiet, humble woman who would feed us and give us some of her special sweet potato pie. She moved to the Grimball Plantation during the 1940s.

Many of Virginia's descendants still live on James Island.

Virginia "Mama" Brown Champagne. *Courtesy of Annabelle Brown.*

Frederick and Emily Deleston Champagne

Frederick Champagne was born in 1899 and died in 1932. His wife, Emily Deleston Champagne, was born in 1900 and died in 1968. Frederick was the grandson of William (1842) and Rebecca Champagne (1845). They were slaves and sharecroppers on the Dill Plantation. Emily was the daughter of Pricilla Deleston (1876), the granddaughter of Joseph (1838) and Dolly Frazier Deleston (1838), and the great-granddaughter of Frank (1810) and Rosa Deleston (1815).

After his marriage to Emily, Frederick moved to the Grimball Plantation, where his wife Emily lived. Emily was a member of St. James Presbyterian Church. Frederick was employed by the Charleston County government to work on a Folly Road project in 1932. Part of the road caved in, and he was killed instantly.

During conversations with Marie Smalls, Emily's granddaughter, she said:

> *Son, my grandmother was my Mama. She raised me and many of her other grandchildren. She was a beautiful black woman within and without, with a lot of love for God and people. Every day if Mama was not talking about God to us, she was singing songs that were about God. She would always say, "My child remember, you can depend on God when you can't depend on nobody else." She would say, "Keep God in your life, praise, and serve him." It's what she taught us that keep my family strong today. God, I miss my Mama! If ever a time I need to hear her voice, it is now in these troubling times.*

Above, left: Frederick Champagne. *Courtesy of Argentina Richardson.*

Above, right: Emily Deleston Champagne. *Courtesy of Argentina Richardson.*

I was raised on Grimball Plantation in the community where Emily lived. My father and Emily were cousins. One of her sons, Earl, and I went to school together.

Many of Frederick and Emily's descendants still live on James Island.

Ruth Hamilton

Ruth Hamilton was born in 1911 and died in 2003. Her husband, Ben "Daddy" Hamilton, was born in 1903. Ben was the son of Paul "Commodore" (1863) and Mariah Hamilton (1863). The family lived and worked on the Dill Plantation during the sharecropper and farming era.

During an interview with Catherine Hamilton Grant, Ruth's granddaughter, she said:

> *Son, I was raised by my grandmother, Ruth. She told me that her parents died when she was an infant and her sister Neomi was too young to take care of her so Joe and Lizzy Deleston adopted and raised her on the Dill Plantation during the time Park Mikell was manager of the farm.*

She continued:

> *She met and married my grandfather, Ben, at a young age. Everyone in the community called him by his nickname of "Daddy." My grandmother worked in Summerville for several years. Later, she got a job working for the Charleston County Public School cafeteria system and worked there for over thirty years before she retired. My grandfather worked at the Charleston Naval Shipyard for several years but died before he retired. Besides working on their jobs, they had a farm where they grew vegetables to feed the family and sell on the Charleston Market. This would help them buy the land where many of the family live today. Son, my grandmother loved to farm, make homemade wine, bake and jar foods.*
>
> *When I was growing up, every Sunday, we had to attend Sunday school and church and pray service throughout the week. She taught us how to work hard and pay our bills, even if we only had a penny left in our pocket after our bills was paid, and to appreciate what we have even if it is a matchbox. We were not allowed to play with other children's toys or borrow anything. She said if you do not have any, wait until you can afford to*

Ruth Hamilton. *Courtesy of Catherine Hamilton Grant.*

get it. Also while growing up, we were not allowed to disrespect an adult, if you did you would get a spanking from that person, and when you got home, you would get another beating from your parents.

She would often tell me how she had to catch a ferry from the boat landing to Mount Pleasant to buy flour and rice. At an earlier age, she taught me how to shop and pay bills for the household. She would give me the grocery list and $25 to shop at Leon's Grocery Store downtown on Spring Street in Charleston. As you already know, when we were young we had to walk to school. Everyone had what we consider a set of dress clothes that we wear to church and special functions. When you get home, you take it off and hang it up for the next Sunday. I remember we went in the woods and cut those tall grass straws and my grandmother would tie them together and make a broom to sweep the floor. This was the way we were raised here on James Island and is proud of all of our accomplishments.

Many descendants of Ruth and Ben still live on James Island.

Alfred Smalls

Alfred Smalls was born in 1894. He was married to Rosa Gladden Smalls. Alfred was the grandson of slaves Jake "Jacob" (1798) and Violet Smalls (1810). He was born and raised on the Dill Plantation, where he and his family were farmers and sharecroppers. He was also a carpenter.

An unknown pilot flying over Turkey Penn from the Carolina Skyways Airport once located on Riverland Drive took the picture of Alfred shown here pushing a planter's plow, which was often referred to as a horseless plow, planting seeds on his farm. This farm was once located where the Meridian Housing Complex now stands on Riverland Drive,

Alfred Smalls. *Courtesy of Evelyn Urie Forest.*

adjacent to and behind the Nativity Catholic Church on Folly Road. This picture was taken sometime during the late 1940s. I remember his farm as being in the same general area where my grandfather lives in the Turkey Pen area of the Dill Plantation. Many of Alfred's descendants still live on James Island.

Mary "Feedie" Champagne Roper

Mary "Feedie" Champagne Roper was born in 1888 and died in 1989. Her daughter, Viola, was born in 1925. Mary was the granddaughter of William (1842) and Rebecca Champagne (1845) of the Dill Plantation, where they were slaves, sharecroppers and farmers.

Mary "Feedie" Champagne Roper.
Courtesy of Viola R. Richardson.

In 1912, Mary married James Roper, and they moved to the Grimball Plantation, where her husband was also a farmer. Mary was known as and affectionately called "Cousin Feedie" by everyone in the community who knew her. She was a midwife and received her medical training at the Medical Health Institute in Sumter, South Carolina. According to Mary, and many people who knew her, she delivered over one thousand babies in the Charleston area during her midwife career. This number included many white babies. She was considered one of the black matriarchs on James Island.

I recall on one occasion during the 1970s, giving Mary a ride home in an unmarked police car from the senior citizens center located at St. James Presbyterian Church on the corner of Fort Johnson and Secessionville Road. During the trip, she said:

> *Boy, let me make you laugh. One summer day, I think it was in 1922, my sons, Ned and Morris, was playing in the yard when they come running in the house yelling that there was a horse coming down the road with no head! My husband and I went outside to see what the boys were yelling about. Going down the one lane dirt road, Grimball Road, was one of them little T Model pickup truck heading toward the Grimball Plantation house. The boys had never seen a car or truck before and call the truck a horse with no head on it! Me and my husband Jim had a good laugh about it for some time.*

Many descendants of Mary and James Roper still live on James Island.

Benjamin and Martha Richardson

Benjamin Richardson was born in 1915 and died in 1971. He was married to Martha Richardson (1917). Benjamin was the son of Cornelius Sr. (1896) and Margaret Richardson (1900) and the grandson of Limus

(1862) and Betty E. Richardson (1860). Martha was the daughter of Joe (1881) and Lizzy Smalls Deleston (1893–1964) and the granddaughter of Joseph (1838) and Dolly Frazier Deleston (1838).

Benjamin Richardson. *Courtesy of Martha R. Green.*

Benjamin was known by his nickname "Ben," and Martha was known by her nickname "Love" by the people in the community. Ben was a member of St. James Presbyterian Church. He had a baritone voice and sang in the church choir. I recall on several occasions sitting in church as a teenager listening as Ben sang, "Sun Rise Tomorrow." He would mesmerize the congregation.

Hettie Gadsden Prioleau

Hettie Gadsden Prioleau. *Family photographs.*

Hettie Gadsden Prioleau was born in 1872 and died in 1986. She was married to Walter Prioleau Sr., who was born in 1871 and died in 1949. Hettie was the daughter of slaves, Joseph (1838) and Charlotte Johnson Gadsden (1840), and the granddaughter of Francis (1816) and Hannah Gadsden (1820), all of whom resided on the Dill Plantation.

After Hettie married Walter, they moved to the Grimball Plantation to become farmers. Hettie was 114 years old when she died in 1986. During one of my conversations with Hettie, she said:

> *Son, my aunt Peggy Gadsden* [1831–1895] *and her daughter Lydia Gadsden* [1859] *was injured in the 1893 storm. Peggy's house was pick up off its foundation and thrown to another part of the Dill Plantation. I don't think they ever fully recover before they died.*

This information was corroborated and substantiated by several people, including my grandmother, Mary Chavis Frazier (1880), and Frank Deleston (1875), as well as by information obtained from the local archives. Hettie was the grandmother of Francis Prioleau Frazier, my wife. We lived with Hettie and her family for the first six months of our marriage. Many of Hettie and Walter's descendants still live on James Island.

Thomas Jr. and Theresa Middleton

Thomas Middleton Jr. was the son of slaves, Thomas (1850) and Rachel Middleton (1865). He was the grandson of Thomas (1808) and Flora Middleton (1825). Thomas's father, Thomas Middleton Sr. (1850), was one of the state constables in the Hunter Hall Lodge on James Island following slavery. Thomas Jr. was married to Theresa M. Middleton.

During a conversation with Thomas, he said:

> *Frazier, my aunt Janie raised my brothers, sister and me. I left Charleston in 1940, during World War II, and joined the U.S. Navy. At the end of the war, I ended up living in Boston, Massachusetts. When I was a young*

Thomas Jr. and Theresa Middleton.
Courtesy of Thomas Middleton.

boy, I used to caddy for white men on the golf course in Charleston and became interested in the sport. There were no golf courses for blacks in Charleston, and segregation was rigidly enforced in the South.

He continued:

I became associated with the Franklin Park Golf Course in the 1950s. While living in Boston, I competed in tournaments throughout the region, occasionally traveling as far as Miami. In 1958, I became the first African American to win the championship at the course. I won again the following year after playing the course for over a decade.

After he retired, Thomas and his wife returned home to South Carolina, where they lived on James Island, the place where Thomas was born and raised. Thomas's wife, Theresa, is deceased, and he is a member of St. James Presbyterian Church. Many descendants of the Middleton family still live on James Island.

James Smalls

James "Scoot" Smalls. *Courtesy of Rene Smalls.*

James Smalls was born in 1916 and died in 1999. James is the brother of my mother, Viola Smalls Frazier. He was married to Susie Lemon Smalls, who was born in 1920 and died in 2004. James was the son of slaves Daniel (1853–1954) and Lucy Todd Smalls and the grandson of slaves, Jake "Jacob" (1798) and Violet Smalls (1810). The Smalls were slaves, sharecroppers and farmers on the Dill Plantation in the area referred to as Turkey Penn. James's parents and grandparents are buried at the Dill Slave Cemetery on the Dill Plantation.

After he married his wife, Susie, James left the Dill Plantation. He and his family moved to the Fort Johnson area. He worked as a delivery salesman for the Rhode Lumber Company, which later became the Buck Lumber Company on Maybank Highway, until his retirement. He was a member of the First

Baptist Church on Camp Road. He was also one of the original fifty-six men who helped organize the Sons of Elijah Masonic Lodge on James Island in 1955.

Three of James and Susie's daughters—Loretta S. Chisolm, Rene Smalls and Lucille S. Hudson, who returned home from New York after her retirement—still live in the house that James and Susie built in the Fort Johnson area on James Island.

Miley Urie

Miley Urie was born in 1854, and her husband, Hump Urie Sr., was born in 1844. Miley was Native American and lived on the Kiawah Island Reservation with her family. According to her grandson, Harry Urie, she was attending an Indian festival with her parents and sibling at the place now known as Angel Oak, located off Bohicket Road on Johns Island, when they were kidnapped by white men. She was sold to the Dill Plantation, where she worked, met and married Hump Urie, Sr.

Miley Urie. *Courtesy of Mary Urie Washington.*

During one of my conversations with Harry over the years, he said:

> *Son, following slavery and during the sharecropping and farming time, my grandmother, Miley, tried to find her mother and her sibling who were sold to other plantations during slavery, but she never found them before she died. I believe my grandmother died from a broken heart.*

Miley and her husband are buried at the Dill Slave Cemetery on the Dill Plantation. Many descendants of Miley and Hump Urie still live on James Island.

Harry Urie Sr.

Harry Urie Sr. was born in 1916 and died in 2002. His wife, Florence Urie, was born in 1923. Harry was the son of Janie Urie Gadsden (1896), the stepson of Joseph Gadsden (1894) and the grandson of slaves, Miley (1854) and her husband, Hump Urie Sr. (1844).

Harry Urie Sr. *Courtesy of Janet Urie White.*

Harry was a mulatto. His father was Edward "Neddie" Grimball (1882–1960), a white plantation owner from Johns Island. Harry served in the United States Army during World War II. During one of our interviews, Harry said:

> *Son, after my discharge from the army, Neddie sent for me and gave me $5,500 to get started in life. I used the money to build my first house in Fergerson Village. Neddie sent for me the second time in 1960 but died before I got to see him. He did explain to me that during the early 1900s, those were still difficult times and, although my mother was a good woman, blacks were not accepted in the white race.*

Janet Urie White. *Courtesy of Janet Urie White.*

Harry was a self-made carpenter and built his own house and the popular Little Rock Golf Club for Richard Smalls, who was instrumental in building the Six Hole Golf Course on Grimball Road during segregation so that black men would be able to play the game. I considered Harry a historian because of his vast knowledge of the history of James Island. Several of Harry's children and grandchildren still live on land he bought in the Fergerson Village and Turkey Pen areas on James Island.

Janet Urie White

Janet Urie White is the daughter of Harry and Florence Urie and the granddaughter of Janie (1896) and her husband, Joseph Gadsden (1894). She is also the great-granddaughter of slaves, Miley (1854) and Hump Urie (1844).

During our interview, Janet said:

> *Frazier, my father, Harry Urie Sr., was a caring and loving father and grandfather. He was also my best friend. He made sure his children always came first in his life. This is a lesson he taught us early in our childhood. Although, it is customary to serve guests first when they visit your home, my daddy made sure his children ate first. He raised us equally with a stern hand ensuring that we had all the necessary values to be great at whatever we did. Some may say he was stricter on the boys. Even though our childhood may have seemed tough, I now know that the challenges we had helped to sculpt the person I am today.*

She continued:

> *Daddy was just preparing us for the future and I thank him for it every day. With the difficult times he had growing up, he made sure we lived a better life than he could have ever imagined. His devoted faith and belief in the church was, without question, the foundation that kept him grounded. Once Daddy didn't allow us to have friends over or even leave the yard if we hadn't gone to church. We wouldn't even think about going to the Juke Joint either. Daddy wouldn't have any of that. It is tough to argue that his upbringing wasn't the force that led most of his five sons and one of his daughters to serve honorably in the military.*
>
> *Despite the ongoing dangers of the war, they went, and the toughness they learned growing up brought them all home. Limited education didn't stop this smart man from being a carpenter, plumber, gardener and whatever else he put his mind to being. All of his children learned the skills he taught us to build a stable home. We also inherited his desire to nurture a wonderful family, too. Daddy was a man that stood by his word and practiced what he preached. Not a day goes by where I don't think of our relationship. I will proudly live my life as if he is right by my side because I know he is watching me, and I know he is proud of who I am.*

Janet, her sister, her brother and many relatives still live on James Island.

Daniel and Bernice Black Stewart

Top: Daniel Stewart. *Courtesy of Bernice Stewart.*

Bottom: Bernice Black Stewart. *Courtesy of Bernice Stewart.*

Bernice Black Stewart was born in 1916. Her husband, Daniel Stewart, was born in 1914 and died in 1958. Bernice was the daughter of Holling (1890) and Bessie Hamilton Black (1896), and the granddaughter of Noah Black (1860). Daniel was the son of William (1876) and Julia Stewart (1885), and the grandson of slaves Lewis (1849) and Ameritta Legg Stewart (1854).

During conversations with Elizabeth Brisbane, the youngest daughter of Bernice and Daniel Stewart, she said:

Frazier, as a young girl growing up my mother was very attentive to us. She took us to Sunday school and church every Sunday. She also made sure that we got to and from school safely. She believed that her children should get a good education. Even though she worked outside the home as a domestic worker, she made sure her family was well cared for. She believed that children should be disciplined if needed.

She continued:

I remember some of the nice things she did for us like surprising us with gifts without any reason and buying my sisters beautiful clothes. My sister, Loretta, and I would be dressed alike. My parents brought the family up in a strong, stable environment with good moral values. My mother was a kind, loving and compassionate women. She loved her family and was loved dearly by them. Like the saying goes, you can pick your friends but not your family. I wouldn't change being her daughter, even if I could. That is how much she means to me and my siblings.

Many of Bernice and Daniel Stewart's descendants still live in the Cut Bridge section of James Island.

Robert Gladden

Robert Gladden was born in 1902 and died in 1979. He was married to Elouise Gladden, who was born in 1904 and died in 1969. Robert was the son of slaves James (1838) and Betsey Gadsden Gladden (1856). Robert and Elouise were members of the St. James Presbyterian Church, and Robert also served on the deacon board.

James Gladden (1838) was a mulatto and one of the overseers on the Dill Plantation during the slavery, sharecropping and farming eras. Robert was born on the Dill Plantation in the place known as Ficken, which is now part of the area where the Municipal Golf Course is located

From left: Robert Gladden; his daughter, Lillian Gladden Washington; and his wife, Elouise Gladden, working in their farm, which was located on Scott Hill Road off Grimball Road. *Courtesy of Lillian Gladden Washington.*

between Riverland Drive and Fleming Road. The area where Robert and his family are working in the accompanying photo is where his daughter, Lillian Gladden Washington, lives today. Many descendants of Robert and Elouise Gladden still live on James Island.

Thomas Walton Jr.

Thomas Walton Jr. *Courtesy of Josephine R. Walton.*

Thomas Walton Jr. was born in 1923 and died in 2004. He was married to Josephine D. Walton, who was born in 1928. Thomas was the son of Thomas Sr. (1875) and Livinia Singelton Walton (1888), and the grandson of slaves Daniel (1840) and Tena Walton (1842). Josephine was the daughter of Joe (1881) and Lizzy Smalls Deleston (1893) and the granddaughter of Joseph (1838) and Dolly Frazier Deleston (1838).

During one of my conversations with Thomas over the years, he said:

> *Frazier, let me tell you, I was raised just like many of the young boys growing up on James Island. Our parents strongly believed in God and prayer. When I was a young boy growing up, my brothers and I had a lot of chores to do. I went to Cut Bridge School about a mile from here on Riverland Drive. The school was sitting in the marsh by a small bridge and at one time the road was called Stono Road.*
>
> *After I finished elementary school, there were no high schools on James Island for black people. The black people that wanted a high school education had to attend Burke Industrial High School in the City of Charleston. Frazier, during my time growing up, it was not easy getting to school in the city from James Island. Sometime, we were lucky and caught rides with the few black people that owned cars on James Island; otherwise, we had to walk to school. I worked for the Charleston Naval Shipyard and retired after working there for thirty-seven years.*

Thomas was a member and elder of the St. James Presbyterian Church, one of the original founders of the Sons of Elijah Masonic Lodge #457 on James Island and the lodge's second elected worshipful master. He was also one of the worthy patrons to the daughters of the Eastern Star #337. Thomas was considered one of the pillars in the community. Many of Thomas's relatives still live on James Island.

Isaac Kinlock

Isaac Kinlock was born in 1901 and died in 2006. He was married to Mary Kinlock, who was born in 1903. Isaac was the son of John (1876) and Lucy Kinlock (1878), and the grandson of slaves, John Sr. (1845) and Eliza Kinlock (1847).

My interviews with Isaac took place over a three-year period. In one of those interviews, he said:

Isaac Kinlock. *Courtesy of Dorothy Kinlock.*

> *Son, I was born and raised on the Dill Plantation. From the time I was a boy, I worked on the farm plowing, digging up Irish potatoes, picking cotton, beans and tomatoes. This was during the time when Fuller King and Park Mikell ran the Dill farm. When I reach twenty-five years old, I went to work for the Charleston County government and drive tractors and heavy equipment clearing roads on James Island.*
>
> *Son, I also had my own farm that my family and me worked. I had a small truck, and I haul my vegetables to the Charleston Market on Meeting Street to sell. That is where the rest of the black farmers took their vegetables. Son, them was hard time in our life, but we work hard and believed in God and pray. We come a long way. This young generation would never be able to stand the trial and tribulations we went through. Son, I remember your great-granddaddy Cyrus Frazier. He was one of them root doctor and when the people on the Dill plantation got sick, they would go to Cyrus' house on Grimball Plantation for their medicine. The slaves say that Cyrus's daddy teach him the medicine trade that he bring from Africa.*

During an interview with Dorothy Kinlock, the daughter of Isaac, she said:

> *Son, I was born and raised on Turkey Pen, by my father and mother. From a very young age they instilled in my sister and brothers to stand on our own two feet, to place God in front of our life and to treat everyone the way we want to be treated. That is how we were raised. I left James Island in 1948, and went to New York to make a better life for myself.*

She continued:

> *I retired after working for the U.S. Postal service in New York for forty years. I returned home in 1988, and worked for the* Post & Courier Newspaper *for fourteen years before I quit. After my father became sick, I took care of his every need until he died in 2006, at the age of 105. My house here in Queenboro is less than five hundred yards from where my brother, sister, and me was born and raised in Turkey Pen on James Island.*

Another daughter, Florence Kinlock Connell, said:

> *Frazier, I left home in 1947, to seek better opportunities. I ended up in Brooklyn, New York. I worked as a school aide for 25 years and retired. In 1996, I came back home to James Island where I was born and raised by a loving father and mother. I remember times when I was a young girl; my father would drive me and my sister around in his T-Model Ford and whenever we passed boys on the dirt roads we would push down in the seat so they could not see us. Bubba, that was our Daddy's nickname, told us that if we did that again he would stop and let us out in front of the boys.*

Many of Isaac's descendants still live on James Island.

Lillian Gladden Washington

Lillian Gladden Washington was born in 1925. Her husband is Morris Washington Sr. Lillian is the daughter of Robert (1902–1979) and Elouise Gladden (1904–1969), and the granddaughter of slaves James (1836) and Betsy Gadsden Gladden (1856–1931).

During our conversations over the years, Lillian said to me:

Lillian Gladden Washington. *Family photograph.*

Gene, I was born and raised on the Dill Plantation in the section called Ficken. It is the area where the Municipal Golf Course is now located. It was during the time when Fuller King managed the plantation. My grandfather, James Gladden [1836] *was one of the overseers on the plantation during that time. As a young girl growing up, I worked on the farms throughout my teenage youth. I attended Cut Bridge Elementary, Society Corner and Burke High Schools in Charleston. As an adult, I worked at the American Tobacco Company "Cigar Factory" for twenty-four years before it shut down in 1962. I took nurse's aide training at the Medical College Hospital, now known as MUSC. After retiring from MUSC, I worked for the state with the Department of Social Services in their adult care program until I was unable to work anymore.*

She continued:

Gene, while growing up, my father taught me about morals, worshipping God, our Lord and Savior, Jesus Christ and the importance of the church in our family life. As a young woman, my father taught me how to ride horses, and play the game of golf. He was an avid golfer and loved the game. He was among the first group of black men on James Island to play the game. I thank God for a wonderful husband, Morris, two daughters, Barbara Forrest Boston, and Kathleen Forrest McFall, a son Morris Washington Jr., a daughter Mary Forrest Middleton, and a son Willie Forrest Jr., who preceded me in death. I became a member of St. James Presbyterian Church at a young age and am presently serving as a deacon and division leader.

Lillian and many of her family still live on James Island.

Edward "Moss" Drayton

Edward "Moss" Drayton. *Courtesy of Kerzel Drayton.*

Edward "Moss" Drayton was born in 1899. He was married to Louise T. Drayton. Edward was the son of slaves, John (1850) and Jane Smalls (1855). John and Jane were slaves, sharecroppers and farmers on the Hinson Plantation.

Edward moved to the McLeod Plantation in the section called "the Hill." During an interview with Kerzel Drayton Fleming, the daughter of Edward "Moss" Drayton, she said:

> *Frazier, where we used to live when I was a young child is not far from where I live here today on Flint Street. There were a lot of peach and pear trees on "the Hill." As you know during the 1900s throughout the 1930s, the majority of black men on James Island were farmers, and time was hard for everyone. But our parents raised us to believe in and pray to "God" that if you treat people the way you want to be treated then everything would be alright.*

Many of Edward and Louise's descendants still live on James Island.

William "Buster" Seymour Sr.

William "Buster" Seymour Sr. was born in 1915. His wife, Ethel Seymour, was born in 1918. William was the son of Daphne Sanders (1888) and William Seymour (1880) and the grandson of slaves Alex (1848) and Tena Seymour (1857). William was affectionately called "Buster" by the people in his community. He was a member of the St. James Presbyterian Church on James Island, where he served on the trustee and usher boards.

During a conversation with Kerzel Drayton Fleming (1924), she said:

William "Buster" Seymour Sr. *Courtesy of Leonard Seymour.*

> *Frazier when I was a young girl the children used to call Buster's mother "Aunt Minnie." I never did know her real name. She used to live near Cut Bridge School at the corner of Riverland Drive and Camp. I remember she was a midwife and went to deliver babies in the community whenever she was needed. She used to give the children a nickel a piece to buy candy from Tucker's Store which was a one-story board building that was located on the corner of Camp and Riverland Drive.*

Many descendants of the Seymour family still live in the Cut Bridge section of James Island.

Arthur Brown

Arthur Brown was born in 1909. He was married to Mae De Brown. Mr. Brown was the son of Arthur (1884) and Clara Brown (1886), and the grandson of Julia Fergerson Brown (1865). Arthur was a prominent businessman in the Charleston area involved primarily in the real estate sector. He was a civic leader in the community for decades and president of the local chapter of the NAACP for several years before and during integration.

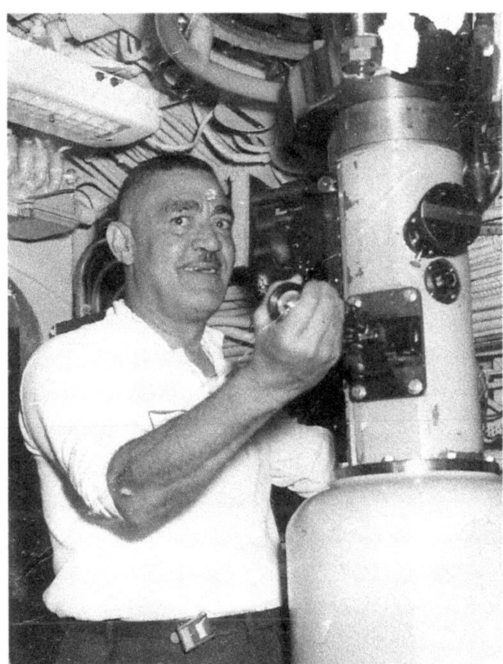

Arthur Brown aboard the submarine *Carver* of the Sixth Naval District in 1966, at the invitation of the admiral. *Courtesy of Gregg Brown.*

He was credited with filing the first civil rights lawsuit in Charleston on behalf of his daughter, Millecent E. Brown. His lawsuit charged the Charleston County school board with racial discrimination in reference to the education of black students. This lawsuit would later be combined with others, including one filed in Topeka, Kansas, which would become known as *Brown v. the Board of Education*. The decision overturned *Plessy v. Ferguson*, which stated that separate but equal schools were unconstitutional. The trial was held in the federal district court at the corner of Broad and Meeting Streets in Charleston, South Carolina. Many relatives of Arthur Brown still live on James Island.

Hester Fell Palmer

Hester Fell Palmer. *Courtesy of Jacqueline W. Young.*

Hester Fell Palmer was born in 1876. Her husband, Royal Palmer was born in 1860 and died in 1935. Hester was the daughter of slaves, Elizabeth Fell (1842) and Amos Prioleau (1838). Elizabeth was a descendant of Daniel (1823) and Sarah Fell (1830–1934). At the time of her death, Sarah Fell was the oldest surviving slave on James Island.

The Fells were slaves and sharecroppers on the Dill Plantation. Royal Palmer lived and worked on the Sol Legare Plantation. Many of Hester and Royal's descendants still live in the Sol Legare area on James Island.

Daniel Smalls

On numerous occasions when I was between five and six years old, my grandpa Daniel Smalls would place me on his shoulders with my legs straddled around his neck. He would use a long piece of oak wood as a pole and tell me to hold on. He would wade through water that sometimes reached his shoulder, depending on how high the tide was. There was a rope tied to a bush on the opposite side that stretched across the small canal. The canal traveled east under Folly Road, followed a path across the island and emptied into the Ashley River. This rope was used for people to hold

Above, left: Eugene Frazier, the author, standing by the canal that ran from the Stono River under Riverland Drive through the Dill Plantation to Folly Road. The site of the canal is adjacent to where the First Federal Bank and the Walmart Store now stand. *Courtesy of the* Post & Courier.

Above, right: Grave marker of Daniel Smalls (1853–1954). *Courtesy of Eugene Frazier Sr.*

on to keep from drowning. Sometimes we used this route as a shortcut to reach the Grimball Plantation instead of walking the dirt road, which was approximately three miles longer.

Daniel Smalls was born in 1853 and died in 1954. His wife, Lucy Todd Smalls, was born in 1858 and died in 1940. Daniel and his parents, Jake (1798) and Violet Todd Smalls (1810), were slaves. Daniel was the private chauffeur for Joseph T. Dill (1822–1900) and drove him and his family around the plantation in a horse and buggy. He would also drive his daughters, Francis and Pauline, to school. This was during the late 1800s and early 1900s. Joseph Dill died in 1900, and Fuller King became manager of the plantation. Daniel became the chauffeur for him prior to the days of the automobile and truck.

After slavery, Daniel became a sharecropper and farmer on the Dill Plantation. I remember my grandfather being a physically strong and mentally sharp man. When I left home to join the U.S. Army during the Korean War, my grandfather was ninety-nine years old and was still walking around in the community. He died while I was stationed in Korea, but I was unable to attend his funeral. All of my maternal grandparents and great-grandparents, a sister and a brother are buried at the slave cemetery on the Dill Plantation.

Estel Roper Champagne

Estel Roper Champagne.
Courtesy of Arthur Champagne Jr.

Estel Roper Champagne was born in 1897 and died in 2003. Her husband, Arthur Champagne, was born in 1896. Estel was the daughter of Samuel (1871–1939) and Elsey Roper (1873–1950). They were sharecroppers and farmers on the Dill Plantation.

In addition to farming, I recall that Estel and her husband operated a small, one-room wooden store on Riverland Drive that was famous for selling link sausages from the 1940s until the late 1950s. Estel was known for smoking her pipe, and her husband was known for smoking a pipe and cigars. The store was located across the road from King Solomon Lodge Hall on the Dill Plantation on Riverland Drive. Many of Estel's descendants still live on James Island.

William "Bill" and Winifred Cribb

William "Bill" Cribb was born in 1919, and his wife, Winifred Cribb, was born in 1923. Winifred was the daughter of Roland Victor Church (1890) from England and Ethel West Church from Atlanta, Georgia. During an interview, Mrs. Cribb said:

> *Frazier, my father was known as the "Dare Devil Race Driver from Atlantic, Georgia." He was well known throughout the south during the 1940s. After Bill and I got married in 1944, we moved to James Island into a board house on Riverland Drive where the Carolina Skyway Airport once was located on the Dill Plantation.*

She continued:

> *During that period, the airport was managed by William Scott to train Citadel cadets to fly prior to entering military service. Bill went to work for Ellinson Brokerage on the dock in Charleston. I recall when the company's building caught on fire. I drove the pickup truck to the job looking for him until I found out that he was safe. Bill worked for the*

William "Bill" Cribb and Winifred Cribb. *Courtesy of Winfred Cribb.*

Above, left: William "Billy" Cribb Jr., standing beside a Piper Cub airplane at the Carolina Skyway Airport, once located on Riverland Drive on the Dill Plantation. *Courtesy of Winifred Cribb.*

Above, right: William "Bill" Cribb Sr. (1919) in his army airborne uniform, complete with his parachute, during World War II. *Courtesy of Winifred Cribb.*

Brokerage Company until they went out of business. After that, he went into the business of farming.

While we were living on the airport property, Bill did part-time maintenance work on the small Piper Cub Airplane for William Scott, flying and keeping them ready to fly for many years. My children were riding in airplanes with their father before they learned to walk. Bill became the caretaker for the Dill Plantation until he retired. We also operated a small grocery store on the corner of Folly Road and Grimball Road for several years until I retired. I came out of retirement and worked for another thirty-seven years for Charleston Supply Company. I also drove school buses for Charleston County two years prior to the state using students to drive buses.

William "Billy" Cribb Jr.

William "Billy" Cribb Jr. was born in 1944 and died in 1974. He was the son of William and Winifred.

William "Billy" Cribb, Jr. was a patrolman with the Charleston County Police Department. In November 1974, during an armed robbery at Sam's Red & White Supermarket, located on the corner of Camp and Folly Roads on James Island, he was shot and killed. He made the ultimate supreme sacrifice. He gave his life in the line of duty, thereby continuing the tradition of numerous police officers who give their lives unselfishly in order to protect and defend the public. I was one of the detectives assigned to investigate the robbery and murder. Tragically, the murder of William "Billy" Cribb Jr. remains unsolved. Mrs. Cribb and some of her family still live on James Island.

George Nungenzer Jr.

The section of the Civil War Historical Fortified Battery located on Riverland Drive is one of several sections left on James Island. This section of the battery can still be seen in the wooded area on Riverland Drive across from where the Carolina Skyways Airport entrance once was. It is located approximately fifty yards south and diagonally across the road from King Solomon Lodge Hall on the Dill Plantation. The Civil War Battery once stretched from the Stono River through the Dill Plantation to the end of Sol Legare at the Stono River.

Section of the Civil War Historical Fortified Battery on Riverland Drive. *Family photograph.*

I recall one day in 1942 walking on the battery with my grandfather, Daniel Smalls. He pointed out a cannonball left behind by Confederate soldiers after the Civil War. In 1948, one of those cannonballs exploded and killed a local farmer's son. The young man was George Nungezer Jr., who was born in 1933. He was beating on the cannonball with a hammer in the Fort Johnson area of James Island when it exploded and killed him. At the time, my father was working on the Nungezer farm. I vividly remember him coming home and breaking the news concerning little George's death. Evidently, little George used to follow my father around on the farm and became attached to him. He was the only child of George Sr. and Mae Nungezer.

Mose Young

Mose Young was born in 1898. His wife, Julia Chisolm Young, was born in 1902. Mose was the son of Aaron (1865) and Jane Young (1868), and the descendant of slave Morris Young (1849). Julia was the daughter of Fortune (1864) and his wife, Livinia Chisolm (1867).

Mose Young. *Courtesy of Lloyd Young.*

Mose's parents were sharecroppers and farmers on the Dill Plantation. The Chisolm family were farmers on the Grimball Plantation. Many descendants of Aaron and Jane Young still live on the land he once farmed and owned in the Cut Bridge area of James Island. Many of Julia Chisolm's descendants still live on the land her parents once owned on Grimball Plantation.

Cyrus Pinckney Jr.

Cyrus Pinckney Jr. was born in 1906. His wife was Eleanor Pinckney. Cyrus was the son of Cyrus Pinckney Sr. (1871) and Catherine Pinckney (1872). They were farmers on the Dill Plantation.

During a conversation with Emily Pinckney, Cyrus's daughter, she said:

Cyrus Pinckney Jr. *Courtesy of Harold Pinckney.*

Frazier, our father was a soft-spoken man. He was not much for words, but he was very humble. He was a Christian and a member of the First Baptist Church on James Island. All of his children were Christians too. At an early age, our father became a farmer. He was a very likeable man and was liked by everyone who knew him. He was an obedient man and taught his children to be the same. He was honest, loyal and trustworthy and was always there for his children.

My father brought his children up well and taught them all to love and respect one another. Even today, the honesty, loyalty, trustworthiness, love and respect our father taught us, we have taught our children—his grandchildren. These traits will follow us as long as life last. Our father reared ten children, seven boys and three girls. He taught us honor and how to be proud of ourselves in what we did. He taught his children to be reassured about life, and to really appreciate the beauty of life itself, and above all always be true Christians.

My mother, Viola Smalls Frazier, and Cyrus Pinckney Jr. were second cousins. I recall about 1944, my father, who was also a farmer, had a small farm of about six acres behind our house on Grimball Road. His mule died, and I remember him telling my mother that they would have to use some of the money they had saved to buy a horse from "Tooter." People in the community called Mr. Cyrus Pinckney by his nickname, "Tooter." The horse was red, and it would be the last one I used to plow the field prior to entering the U.S. Army.

Many of Cyrus and Eleanor's descendants still live in the Cut Bridge area of James Island.

William Richardson

William Richardson was born in 1922 and died in 2008. His wife was Anne Luten Richardson. William was the son of Cornelius (1896) and Margaret Richardson (1900), and the grandson of Samuel (1867) and Phyllis Richardson (1875). The Richardsons were farmers on the Dill Plantation.

During my conversations with Mr. Richardson over the years, he said:

> *Frazier, let me tell you a little about me. I was born and raised on James Island. They were six boys and three girls in the family. My family was farmers, and they had ten acres on each side of Camp Road. My brothers and I worked on the farm planting and harvesting the vegetables for our parents to sell on the market to support us during those hard years.*
>
> *I went to Cut Bridge Elementary School just across the road from our house on Camp Road and Riverland Drive. After I finished elementary school, there were no high schools on James Island for blacks during the 1920s, 30s or the 40s. Those of us who wanted a high school education had to attend Burke High School in the City of Charleston. As you know there was no public transportation from James Island to Charleston, and the State of South Carolina refused to furnish school buses for "colored" (that's what white people called blacks during that time). So, we had to walk the five mile from*

William Richardson. *Courtesy of Jada R. Bright.*

where I lived to school. Sometimes we were lucky enough to catch rides with the few blacks that owned cars on the island.

After I finished Burke High School, I attended Voorhees Junior College and received an associate's degree. I received a bachelor of science in agriculture from South Carolina State College in Orangeburg. Frazier, I also studied at Virginia State University and Clemson University and served as a principal and teacher in the public schools for over twenty years.

I was drafted into the United States Army during World War II and spent two years in the jungles of Burma, India. Although I joined the church at a young age, I really learned in the jungles of Burma what it meant to have "faith in God." I will always cherish that experience.

Mr. Richardson was a member of the St. James Presbyterian Church on James Island. Besides being an elder, he held virtually every officer position in the church. I have known Mr. Richardson all of my life. He was one of the pillars of the community and a truly great man. Many of Mr. Richardson's descendants and relatives still live on James Island.

Franklin Gilliard

Franklin Gilliard. *Courtesy of Alberta Jenkins.*

Franklin Gilliard was born in 1904, and his wife, Albertha Gilliard, was born in 1906. Franklin was the son of Levy Gilliard Jr. (1884), and the grandson of slave Levy Gilliard Sr. (1840). During the sharecropping and farming era, Franklin lived and worked on the Dill Plantation, plowing and harvesting vegetables like many of the other men on the farm.

Franklin was a member of First Baptist Church on Camp Road. He was baptized in the river at the public boat landing on James Island. He became an assistant leader in 1958 to the late Charlie Goss (1844). He then became the leader of class number three and the conductor of prayer meetings, which were held twice weekly. In 1960, he was appointed deacon. After working several years on the farm, Franklin worked at the Charleston Naval Shipyard for sixteen years and at the Jewish synagogue for twenty years until he retired.

Franklin owned the property on Riverland Drive located at the front entrance to Fergerson Village. When Franklin learned that families living near his property in Fergerson Village had no way to reach their property, he gave up part of his property so that an access road could be opened. After the road was opened and paved, it was dedicated to him and named Franklin Gilliard Road.

Many of Franklin and Alberta's children still live in the Cut Bridge section of James Island.

James W. Scott

James W. Scott was born in 1915, and his wife, Mary Leize Scott, was born in 1916. James was the son of June (1883) and Albertha Scott. During an interview with James Scott on July 12, 2005, prior to his death, he said:

James W. Scott. *Courtesy of James Scott.*

> *Frazier, when I was a young boy, my brothers, sisters and me all worked on the farms. My brother Israel did not like the farm life so he moved to the city of Charleston when he was young. I started working on the Dill farm when old Man King* [Fuller King] *was running the farm. I plowed with mules, digs potatoes, breaks corn, pick beans and cotton. I worked with men like Franklin Gilliard. He was married to my sister Bertha. Isaac Kinlock and a lot of other men also worked there. We were paid ten cent a day during those years.*
>
> *Your grandpa, Dan Smalls, was Dill's and King's private chauffeur during the farming time—driving them in a horse and buggy around the plantation and driving his daughters to school. Old man Charlie Goss was made foreman after slavery during farming time. One of Charlie's arms was cut off at his elbow by the Dill cotton machine. The people used to call him "Yubber" and "Cowboy Charlie" as he rides his horse around the farm. Jeffery Lemon was brought in by Park Mikell when he took over the farm, and he made him a foreman.*

He continued:

> *I got a job working at the Charleston Naval Shipyard in 1944. I was lucky during the time. It was the best job a black man could hope to get in Charleston and earn a decent wage to support his family. I retired in 1980 from the shipyard after working thirty-seven years.*

Many of James's descendants still live on James Island.

Daniel "Dan" Nowell Sr.

Daniel "Dan" Nowell Sr. *Courtesy of Lottie N. Prioleau.*

Daniel "Dan" Nowell Sr. was born in 1918 and died in 1995. He was married to Ernestine Nowell. Daniel was the son of Peter Sr. (1894), and Molsey Cromwell Nowell (1895–1974). Peter and Molsey were farmers in the Turkey Penn area on the Dill Plantation during the farming and sharecropper era.

Dan, as he was affectionately called by people in the community, did furniture upholstery repair work and was also a carpenter. He taught this trade at the YWCA. Dan also worked for Charleston County as a janitor at Baxter Patrick Elementary School on Grimball Road for many years. He was a member of Riverside Lodge at the intersection of Grimball Road and Riverland Drive. His many hobbies included golfing and fishing. He was also an avid hunter. Many descendants of Daniel and Ernestine Nowell still live on James Island.

Martha "Neely" Young Rivers

Martha "Neely" Young Rivers was born in 1897 and died in 1970. Her husband, Arthur Rivers, was born in 1895. Arthur was the son of George (1872) and Hester Rivers (1875), the grandson of slaves Elias (1839) and Cornella Rivers (1850), and the great-grandson of George (1820) and Chloe Rivers. The Riverses and Youngs were sharecroppers and farmers

Martha "Neely" Young Rivers. *Courtesy of Gloria Rivers.*

on the Dill Plantation. Martha was the daughter of Aron (1865) and Jane Young (1868).

Martha Rivers was the first women ordained as an elder in the St. James Presbyterian Church under the leadership of Reverend Marion Sanders during the 1950s. During this time, it was not popular for women to be leaders in the church. I remember Mrs. Rivers as being a very religious and humble person who would go to great lengths to help anyone in her community. Many descendants of Martha and Arthur Rivers still live in the Cut Bridge area of James Island.

John "Nat" and Esse Smith

John "Nat" Smith was born in 1910, and his wife, Esse Smith, was born in 1914. John was the son of Nathaniel "Nat" (1888) and Liza Smith (1890),

Above, left: John "Nat" Smith. *Courtesy of James "Mickey" Middleton.*

Above, right: Esse Smith. *Courtesy of James "Mickey" Middleton.*

and the grandson of slaves Daniel (1836) and Susannah Smith (1845). John and his wife were farmers on the Dill Plantation.

According to Lillian Washington:

> *Esse was hired by the Cigar Factory (American Tobacco Company) in Charleston and worked with several people from James Island including my parents, Robert and Elouise Gladden, and myself during the 1940s through the 1960s until she retired. Nat was also a farmer. He was a quiet, humble and hardworking man.*

Many of Nat's descendants still live on James Island.

Diana Todd Heyward

Diana Todd Heyward was born in 1907, and her husband, Jeffery Heyward, was born in 1900. Diana was the daughter of Joe (1882)

Diana Todd Heyward. *Family photograph.*

and Alice Middleton Todd (1887), the granddaughter of Peter (1844) and Lilly Todd (1844), and the great-granddaughter of Sefus (1819) and Emma (1822). Jeffery was the son of Joseph (1882) and Carrie Heyward (1886), and the great-grandson of Joe (1844) and Carolina Heyward (1860)

The Todd family were slaves on the Dill Plantation. After slavery, they became sharecroppers and farmers. The Heyward family were slaves on the McLeod Plantation. During the farming era, they moved to the Dill Plantation, where they lived and became farmers. Many of Todd and Heyward descendants still live on James Island.

Ester Goss

Ester Goss was born in 1906. Her husband, Horace Goss, was born in 1905. They were farmers on the Dill Plantation. Horace was the son of John (1877) and Amelia Goss (1888). Horace and Ester were born and raised on the Dill Plantation. They worked on the farm during the time Fuller King and Park Mikell managed the plantation.

Ester Goss. *Courtesy of Barbara Goss Brown.*

During conversations with Lillian G. Washington over the years, she said:

> *Gene, as a young man, my uncle Horace was very high strung and a sharp dresser. He got a job working at the Cigar Factory (American Tobacco Company) with my father, mother, myself and several other people from James Island during the 1940s and 1950s. He worked there until he retired. My Aunt Ester worked on the farm and was a housewife.*

Many descendants of Horace and Ester still live on James Island.

Isaac Washington

Isaac Washington was born in 1901, and his wife, Florence G. Washington, was born in 1911. Isaac was the son of William (1868) and Nancy Washington (1881). Florence was the daughter of Amelia and Ezekiel Gathers (1892). Isaac, like many black men on James Island during this time, was a farmer. In 2007, his daughter, Evelina Washington Walker, paid tribute to her father in "Remembering Our Roots."

Mrs. Walker said:

Isaac Washington. *Courtesy of Isaac Washington.*

> *As a child growing up on James Island, I have many memories of my daddy, momma, sister and brothers. One thing I must say is that Daddy and Momma were true Christians and lovers of the Lord. Every Tuesday and Wednesday night, we all went to prayer meetinghouse to praise the Lord. As a young girl, I was afraid to pray out loud, but when Daddy started singing and calling our name in the song, by the end of that song, we better be on our knee praying. Daddy always said that praying made you stronger in the Lord. We went to Sunday school every Sunday—rain or shine. Easter and Children's Day were always very special. We would get all dressed up to say our speeches. At Christmas, we got to go to the turkey farm to pick our very own turkey. A few days before Christmas, Daddy would kill a hog, cut off the head, clean it real good and guess what? We would have the hog headcheese over grits on Christmas morning. Every Fourth of July, Daddy made us ice cream in the churn. That was the best ice cream. We would eat so much, our heads would hurt. Momma would bake a cake and make Jell-o and my sister Florence would bake the lemon pie. Holidays were never complete without a hay ride.*

She continued:

> *Daddy was also a farmer. I hated the farm, but it made no difference to him. We all had our chores to do after school. Daddy and Uncle Jake often said, "Alright, when school is out, you better come home in a hurry." We didn't always listen. If you saw Daddy or Uncle Jake walking toward you looking real innocent, with their hands hidden behind their back, you better look out. They were hiding a switch. When Daddy got home from the*

market, he would always bring treats for us like oranges, apples, bananas and big bags of roasted peanuts. I could go on and on forever about the special memories I have of Momma and Daddy. I do know that I can speak for my brothers and sisters in that we were truly blessed with two loving and caring parents. Thank the Lord for lending them to us.

Many of Isaac and Florence's descendants still live on James Island.

Mary Duxein Todd

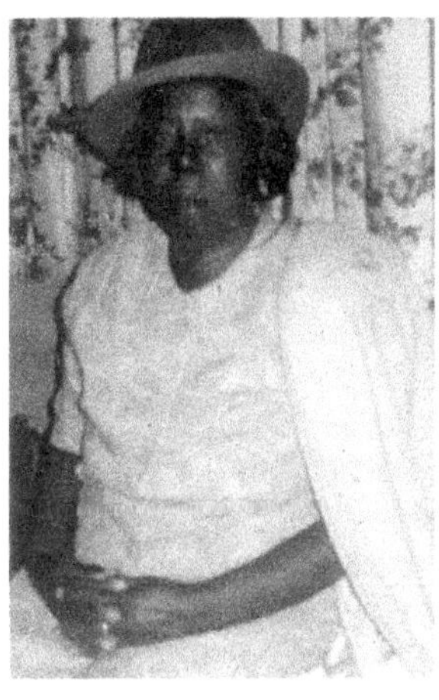

Mary Duxein Todd. *Courtesy of Helen Richardson.*

Mary Duxein Todd was the daughter of sharecroppers, Samson (1820) and Moria Duxein (1825). Mary was married to Primus Todd. Primus was the son of Peter (1844) and Lilly Todd (1844).

In 1883, Samson purchased twenty acres of land from Joseph and Regina Dill for the sum of $400. The land was adjacent to the King Solomon Lodge Hall on Riverland Drive. Mary and Primus were farmers on the Dill Plantation, where they planted many types of vegetables to sell at the Charleston Market on Meeting Street. They also raised hogs and chickens to sell and supplement their income. Many descendants of Mary and Primus still live on James Island. As of this writing, the property is still listed in the estate of Samson Duxein.

Hester "Hesse" Miller

Hester "Hesse" Miller was born in 1909. Hester was the daughter of Louis (1855) and Elizabeth Miller (1875) and the granddaughter of slaves, Captain (1833) and Fanny Miller (1840).

Hester worked on various plantations. She also owned a small farm, where she planted many

Hester "Hesse" Miller. *Courtesy of Dorothy Backman.*

types of vegetables and sold them at the Charleston Market on Meeting Street. She raised chickens and hogs to sell to supplement her income. Her grandson, Larry Backman, helped her on the farm. Many of Hesse's descendants still live on James Island.

James Island Lodges

There was a tradition among the different lodge halls on James Island that when a person died, members would beat the drum and march to the cemetery for the burial. When a member from the King Solomon Lodge on Stono Road (Riverland Drive) died, Joe Deleston (1881), Sandy Frazier Sr. (1880) and Louis Gladden (1878) would beat the drum. Throughout the Grimball Road area from the 1920s to the 1950s, lodge halls in each community also doubled as prayer houses on Tuesday and Thursday nights.

From the 1920s to the 1940s, during the holidays, the men would beat the drum and play the flute and harmonica at the lodge hall for the people to dance. This was the only type of entertainment they had in the community during this time. They used to swing and shag dance. The shag they performed is the same dance that people now call shagging, often accompanied by beach-type music. Each lodge had participants who would march in holiday parades, such as the one held in the city of Charleston on September 6, 1938.

King Solomon Lodge Hall. *Family photograph.*

The Sol Legare Lodge marching band. *From left to right*: Mosey Wilder (1898) beating his drum, Jobe Richardson (1901) playing the flute, Benjamin "Dimmy" Richardson (1898) beating his drum and Wilson Jackson (1900) beating the bass drum. Walking behind them in the parade were Oscar Lafayette (1916), wearing a white hat and dark sunglasses; William Harker (1900), wearing a black hat; and several unidentified men from James Island. This photograph was taken on September 6, 1938. I had the privilege of knowing all of these men and their families personally. *Courtesy of the* Post & Courier.

The King Solomon Lodge Hall was built in 1909 and still stands today in 2009. My father, Sandy Frazier Jr. (1908), was president of the King Solomon Lodge during the 1950s. Sadly, this landmark building, which served African Americans for many decades and remains dear to the hearts of many of the descendants of the original members, was recently sold to a private owner and is undergoing remodeling as of this writing.

I was elected worshipful master of the Sons of Elijah Masonic Lodge #457, Prince Hall Affiliation F&AM, in December 2008. The lodge is located at 1831 Folly Road on James Island. It received its charter as a member of the Prince Hall Grand Lodge in Columbia, South Carolina, in 1955. It now has a membership of 125.

The past masters in the accompanying photos were among the fifty-six men who helped organize the Son of Elijah Lodge on James Island. They were also among its first group of past masters.

Above: Sons of Elijah Lodge #457. *Family photograph.*

Left, clockwise from top left: Past master John Richardson Sr. *Courtesy of Sons of Elijah Masonic Lodge*; Past master Toby Singelton. *Courtesy of Sons of Elijah Masonic Lodge*; Past master Thomas Walton. *Courtesy of Sons of Elijah Masonic Lodge*; Past master James "Brook" William. *Courtesy of Sons of Elijah Masonic Lodge.*

Above, left: Hunter's Hall Lodge. *Family photograph.*

Above, right: Joseph Deleston Jr. *Courtesy Marie Deleston.*

Hunter Hall Lodge is located at the intersection of Grimball Road and Riverland Drive. The original two-story wooden structure was built by slaves during the 1800s. In 1876, the building was used as a voting place for blacks on James Island. During the period following slavery, blacks voted in the Republican Party. The lodge hall was used by the black militia (state constables) to police blacks during the period between the 1800s and 1900s.

The members of the militia after the slavery and sharecropping eras included Isaac Fergerson (1849), captain in charge of the unit; Henry Green, sergeant, second in command; Amos Watson (1848); Thomas Middleton (1850); Charles Knightly (1820); and Julius Richardson (1876). The lodge was renamed Riverside Lodge during the 1900s and served African Americans from the slavery era through the year 2005. This historical landmark was dear to the hearts of African Americans for over two centuries and cherished by their descendants, some of whom still bemoan the loss of the building. Its last president was Joseph Deleston Jr. The building was remodeled for the fourth time by its new owner, Ms. Pricilla Sarpy, and is now a two-story, concrete block building that is used as a beauty salon.

Grimball Plantation

Owners

Henry Grimball was born in 1860 and died in 1943. Henry was married to Lula P. Grimball (1864–1952). Henry was the grandson of Thomas H. Grimball (1682) and Joyce Grimball.

Entrance to the Grimball Plantation. *Family picture.*

Slaves and Their Descendants

Peggy Singelton Whaley. *Courtesy of Levola W. Whaley.*

Daniel and Peggy Singelton Whaley

Peggy Singelton Whaley was born in 1864. Her husband, Henry Whaley, was born in 1861. Henry was the son of Daniel (1833) and Clarissa Whaley (1837). The Whaleys and Singeltons were farmers on the Grimball Plantation. Daniel Whaley was a member of Payne RMUE on Camp Road and is listed as one of the founding fathers who helped build the first church under the leadership of the Reverend Prince "Pappy" White (1830) in 1875.

Charles Whaley

Charles and Blossom Whaley. *Courtesy of Genevieve Lafayette.*

Charles Whaley was born in 1889 and died in 1967. His first wife, Sarah Middleton Whaley, was born in 1895 and died in 1944. Blossom G. Whaley was the second wife of Charles Whaley. His first wife, Sarah, died while attending church service at the St. James Presbyterian Church on Sunday, December 17, 1944.

Charles was the son of Henry Sr. (1861) and Peggy Singelton Whaley (1864) and the grandson of Daniel (1833) and Clarissa Whaley (1837). Sarah was the daughter of Remus Middleton (1856). I attended church services with my father, Sandy Frazier, that Sunday morning in 1944 when Mrs. Sarah Whaley died of an apparent heart attack. It was an experience I will never forget.

Charles and his family were farmers on the Grimball Plantation. He was a deacon

From left to right: Alice Middleton Todd (1887), Janie Middleton Moore (1892), Mary Ann Middleton Chavis (1889) and Sarah Middleton Whaley (1895). *Family photograph.*

and a member of the St. James Presbyterian Church on James Island. Many of the descendants of Charles Whaley still live on James Island.

The Middleton sisters symbolized the essence of togetherness during those difficult years when families understood the importance of giving each other moral, as well as spiritual, support. Each of these beautiful women still has descendants living on James Island.

Catherine Smalls Whaley

Catherine Smalls Whaley was born in 1919 and died in 2001. Her husband, Charles Henry Whaley Sr., was born in 1917 and died in 1955. Catherine was the daughter of Isaac (1892) and Mary Smalls (1896), and the granddaughter of slaves Hector (1846) and Elizabeth Smalls (1846). Henry was the son of Charles (1889) and Sarah Whaley (1895). They all lived on the Grimball Plantation.

During the 1940s and 1950s, when life was hard for African Americans here on James Island, many of them moved to northern states. Catherine and

Catherine Smalls Whaley. *Family photograph.*

her family relocated to New York to make a better life. During conversations over the years, her daughter, Catherine W. Singelton, said:

> *Son, my mother was a woman of substance to all who knew her. She had a big heart and a smile to match. She was a comedian, a storyteller and a people person. There were nine children in the family whom she loved unconditionally. Mother was widowed at a very young age so she was a single mother. She was an excellent seamstress. She taught all of the children to sew, both boys and girls. We learned to cook, clean house and do the laundry. There were no favorites. We were all treated the same. She used to say, "What's good for the goose is good for the gander."*

Mrs. Singelton continued:

> *She believed strongly in education and encouraged us to do our best in school and strive to be productive, strong, and independent adults.*

Mother was not a strict parent, but we knew what was expected, and if it was contrary to her expectations, we would know. She always corrected us with love and wisdom. Mother demanded respect because she gave respect. She traveled extensively throughout the United States and abroad, but her favorite place was home, James Island. She visited often to spend time with friends and family. She didn't drive a car or own one, yet she moved around this island as if she did. She left a lasting impression on everyone she met. Her heart and arms were always open, a daughter, sister, wife, mother, granny, a comedian, people's magnet, but most of all a blessed child of God.

While several of Catherine's family members live in New York, many of her relatives and her daughter returned home to James Island.

Prince "Princy" White

Prince "Princy" White was born in 1866. His wife, Sarah, was born in 1882. Prince was a farmer on the Grimball Plantation but was raised on the Seabrook Plantation, where his father, Middleton (1854), and his grandfather, Prince "Pappy" White (1830), were slaves and overseers on the plantation.

Prince "Princy" White and his wife, Sarah. *Courtesy of Prince Brown.*

Prince and Sarah were farmers on the Grimball Plantation. They grew many different types of vegetables, including corn, okra, green beans, tomatoes, sweet potatoes, collard greens, sugar cane, figs and pear and pecan trees. They also raised cows, hogs, chickens and geese. Prince was affectionately called "Princy." He was a small man, about five feet, four inches tall. He had a red horse and was the first black man I ever saw riding a horse with a saddle during the late 1930s. During this period, we were only accustomed to seeing white farmers riding their saddle horses while trailing their hunting dogs in a pack. Prince was an exception to this rule.

Prince and Sarah lived a short distant down Grimball Road from the Frazier family. According to my grandmother, Mary Chavis Frazier (1880), Prince was one of three men who were injured on James Island during the storm of 1893. Prince and Sarah are buried at the Seabrook slave cemetery on Secessionville Road on James Island. Many of their descendants still live on James Island.

Charlotte Johnson Gathers

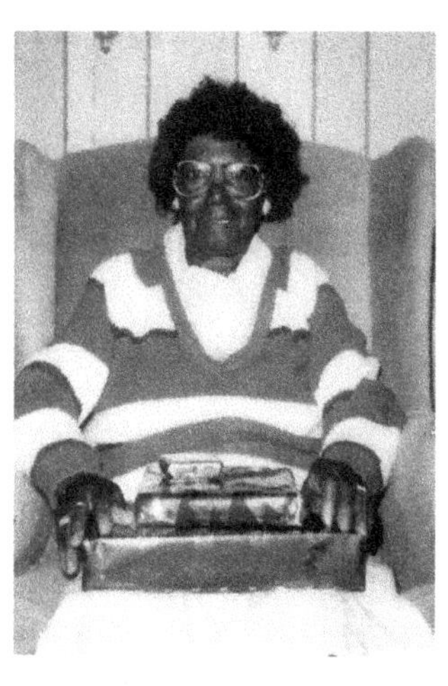

Charlotte Johnson Gathers. *Courtesy of Hanna G. William.*

Charlotte Johnson Gathers was born in 1909 and died in 1990. Her husband, Joseph Gathers, was born in 1911 and died in 1959. Joseph was the grandson of a slave, Hannah Gathers (1836). Charlotte was the daughter of Samuel Sr. (1865) and his wife, Hanna Gadsden Johnson (1868). During her youth, Charlotte worked on various farms like many of the young children. After the death of her husband at the age of forty-eight, Charlotte did domestic work to support her family. She was a member of the St. James Presbyterian Church and the Order of the Eastern Star #337 on James Island. Hannah Gathers (1836) was listed as one of the founding mothers of Payne RUME Church on Camp Road under the leadership of Reverend Prince "Pappy" White (1830). Many of Charlotte's descendants still live on James Island.

Samuel Cromwell

Samuel Cromwell. *Family photograph.*

Samuel Cromwell was born in 1924, and his wife, Mary Cromwell, was born in 1923. Samuel was the son of Allen (1870) and Christine Cromwell (1875) and the grandson of slaves Truman (1854) and Cloranda Cromwell (1855). Mary was the daughter of Sandy Sr. (1889–1939) and Mary Chavis Frazier (1880–1960).

Truman was one of several former slaves who carried lumber on his shoulders, walking from the Seabrook boat landing at Wappoo Creek some two and a half miles along a trail, "Secessionville Road," to the corners of Fort Johnson and Secessionville Road. This location was where the first St. James Presbyterian Church was built in 1868. Truman was one of the founding fathers of the church under the leadership of Reverend H.H. Hunter, who came from the North in 1866 to teach the newly freed slaves to read and write. He also started the first mission school in the church. Many of Truman Cromwell's descendants still live on James Island.

Ellen "Darlin" Middleton

Ellen "Darlin" Middleton. *Courtesy of James "Mickey" Middleton.*

Ellen "Darlin" Middleton was born in 1898. Her husband, Edger Middleton, was also born in 1898. Edger was the son of Mathias Middleton (1866), and the great-grandson of slaves, Cuffie (1790) and Venus Middleton (1810). Ellen was the granddaughter of slaves Daniel (1836) and Susannah Smith (1845). The Smiths were slaves and farmers on the Dill Plantation, and the Middletons were slaves and farmers on the Grimball Plantation. Ellen, who was affectionately called "Darlin," along with her husband, Edger, was a farmer on the Grimball Plantation.

During an interview with Ellen's eldest daughter, Rosalee Middleton Richardson, whom the people in the community affectionately call "Baby," Rosalee said:

> *Son, when my sisters, brother and me were growing up, times was hard. My father and mother had a small farm and grew lots of vegetables, okra, butter beans, string beans, tomatoes, corn and rice. We planted the rice in the lowest part of the land where the water settled. Mama would take the vegetables to the market on Meeting Street in Charleston to sell.*
>
> *To help support the family, we would go with Mama to work picking beans, white potatoes and many other vegetables on the Dill Plantation during the time when it was run by Mr. Fuller King, the Hinson Plantation, when it was run by George Nungezer, and other farms. To help support the family, Papa would go in the creek and catch fish to sell. He also worked on the WPA.*
>
> *Back in them days, Son, the peoples really believe in God—and that he is good all the time. We also helped each other in the community. I had three serious operations to remove one of my kidneys, a hernia, and gallstones while still in my eighties. Son, I am eighty-nine years old and still drive myself to the store and where I need to go. I am blessed and believe in treating people the way I want to be treated.*

Many of Ellen and Edger Middleton's descendants still live on James Island.

Elsey Roper

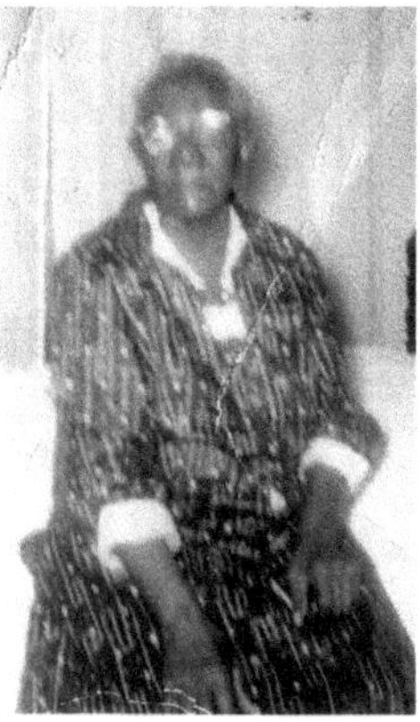

Elsey Roper. *Courtesy of Carrie Middleton.*

Elsey Roper was born in 1873 and died in 1950. Her husband, Samuel Roper Sr., was born in 1871 and died in 1939. Elsey and her husband were sharecroppers and farmers on the Grimball Plantation.

Vegetables grown on the farm during this time included okra, green beans, corn and sweet potatoes. They also raised hogs and chickens and had several fig trees, plum bushes and strawberry plants on their farm. Elsey and her family once lived across the road from the Frazier family and the site of the former Little Rock Golf Club. Many of Elsey and Samuel's descendants still live on James Island.

Samuel and Elsie's children. *From left to right*: Rose Roper (1898), Mary Roper Simmons (1899), Brother Samuel Roper Jr. (1912) and Estell Dell Roper Champagne (1896). *Courtesy of Carrie Middleton.*

Richard Smalls Sr.

Richard Smalls Sr. was a young black man in the 1960s during the time when segregation was still being enforced in Charleston. Richard had spent many years on golf courses and realized that unless a black man was employed as a caddy or as manual labor, he would not be able to play on any golf course in Charleston. Richard decided to do something about this predicament.

Over the years, Richard studied blueprints and plans of golf courses. He also bought eight acres of property adjacent to the Frazier property from Raymond Grimball of the Grimball Plantation. With his nephew Harry Urie, a carpenter, the young entrepreneur built a six-hole golf course and a clubhouse and bar. He named the place Little Rock Golf Club. My brother Jimmie Frazier was employed there as a handyman and bartender from the 1950s until his untimely death in 1967. His death created such a void, but the loving memories that he created with his family and friends have helped to sustain and comfort us throughout the years.

The building was once located at the entrance to the present Little Rock Boulevard on Grimball Road, next door to the Frazier property. Many of

Richard Smalls Sr. *Courtesy of Richard Smalls Jr.*

Eliza Matthew Roper. *Courtesy of Nancy Matthews Washington.*

the black men throughout the metropolitan Charleston area learned how to play the game of golf on the course. Gordon Brown, a young man from James Island, was inducted into the African American Golfer's Hall of Fame on May 29, 2005, in Fort Lauderdale, Florida. He learned to play the game at the Little Rock Golf Course.

Eliza Matthews Roper

Eliza Matthews Roper was born in 1898. She was the daughter of Samuel Matthews (1875) and Nancy Matthews (1878), and the granddaughter of slaves Sam (1830) and Bess Matthews (1823). Eliza's parents were farmers on the Grimball Plantation.

Eliza was known affectionately as "Liza" by the people in the community. In addition to her domestic work, she also owned and operated a small farm. Liza and her family lived next door to the Little Rock Golf Club, which was adjacent to the Frazier property. I remember Liza as a congenial person who would share whatever she had with her neighbors during those trying times.

During a conversation with Elizabeth Matthews, Liza's granddaughter, Elizabeth said:

> *Frazier, early on Eliza was told by her father that she needed to make sure she purchased land to call her own. At that time, the family lived and sharecropped on Grimball Plantation, where her father purchased an overseer's house. She took his advice. She was a dressmaker, a farmer and a domestic worker. She scrimped and saved and was able to purchase six acres of land from Mrs. Lula Grimball to build her home where it still stands today. Eliza was a strong woman who believed in her faith. Her mother died in her thirties, and she was left with her father to care for the family.*

She continued:

> *Her mother had eight girls, and Eliza became the mother to them all. Her older sister Sarah died shortly thereafter, and Eliza was left alone with a father to rear her six sisters. Well remembered, well loved and never forgotten by her family.*

Many of Eliza's descendants still live on James Island.

Paul and Celia Chisolm

Paul Chisolm was born in 1877 and died in 1954. His wife, Celia Chisolm, was born in 1878 and died in 1946. Paul was the son of John (1844–1936) and Rose Chisolm (1846).

Paul and Celia were farmers on the Grimball Plantation. Some of the crops they grew and harvested were green beans, okras, corn, peas, sweet potatoes, tomatoes and strawberries. They also had fig trees, pear trees,

Paul and Celia Chisolm. *Family photograph.*

plum bushes and pecan trees. They raised Jersey cows, hogs, chickens, ducks, geese and turkeys. Like many of the families on James Island, they took the vegetables to the Charleston Market on Meeting Street to sell. Mrs. Celia also grew many different types of flowers in her yard.

The Chisolm family supplied the community with fresh milk every morning from the 1920s through the 1950s. Paul was a member of the St. James Presbyterian Church. He served as an elder, treasurer and class leader. The Frazier family lived across the road from the Chisolms. I remember when Mrs. Celia died in 1946. After her body was prepared by Fielding Home for Funerals, it was brought back to the house for viewing. Many people were able to view her remains before burial. This was the tradition of many families on James Island—to have their loved ones brought back to the house prior to burial.

Many of Paul and Celia's descendants still live on James Island. My wife, Frances Prioleau Frazier, is their granddaughter.

Elouise Frazier

Elouise Frazier was born in 1922. She was the daughter of Sandy Sr. (1880–1939) and Mary Chavis Frazier (1880–1960), the granddaughter of slaves Cyrus (1852–1926) and Rosa Frazier (1852) and the great-granddaughter of Benjamin (1828) and Sibby Frazier (1830).

Elouise, whom I and other family members affectionately call "Aunt Mae," told me:

> *Son, I worked on almost all of the local farms while growing up on James Island. Some include the Grimballs, Dills, Nungezers and Haleys, where I picked beans, tomatoes, broke corn, dug potatoes and picked many more types of vegetables. I also did domestic work for individual homes. I got a job working at the Cigar Factory (American Tobacco Company) in Charleston and worked there for approximately two years as a wrapper putting bands around the cigars before they were shipped to stores.*

She continued:

> *Like many young women from James Island, I left home during those trying times in the 1940s and went to New York to seek better job opportunities to help support our family. I stayed and worked in New York and sent*

Elouise Frazier. *Family photograph.*

> *money back home to Mama. You know Papa died in 1939. In 1960, Mama died, and I came back home to take care of the family. I got a job at the Hunter Frock Company in North Charleston in 1967, working as a seamstress until I retired in 1993.*
>
> *Papa said that after his granddaddy Benjamin arrived on James Island from Africa, he taught his son Cyrus the trade of a root doctor. He taught him to boil certain types of tree roots to make medicine during slavery and the sharecropping and the farming time. Cyrus was the only doctor the slaves on James Island had access to during that era.*

In another conversation that I had with my Aunt Mae and her sister, Eva F. McKelvey (1909–2008), they repeated the fact that in the 1920s, people came knocking on their door asking for Doctor Cyrus, who lived directly behind their house. Elouise is a member of the St. James Presbyterian Church and a former member of the senior choir. Many descendants of the Fraziers still live on James Island.

Joseph Sr. and Emily "Cord" Deleston

Joseph Deleston Sr. was born in 1912 and died in 1968. His wife, Emily "Cord" Deleston, was also born in 1912. Joseph was the son of Frank (1875–1956) and Annie Cromwell Deleston (1878–1948), the grandson of slaves Joseph (1838) and Dolly Frazier Deleston (1838), and the great-grandson of Frank (1810) and Rose Deleston (1815). They were slaves and farmers on the Grimball Plantation.

Joseph (1912) worked for the Charleston County government for several years doing maintenance work on county roads. Joseph and his second wife, Rebecca, were farmers. He was also a self-made barber and cut the hair of many of the men and boys, including my father and me, in the Grimball Road community for many years. Many of the descendants of Joseph and Dolly Deleston still live on James Island.

Eva Frazier Seabrook

Eva Frazier Seabrook was born in 1939. She is married to Charlie Seabrook. Eva is the daughter of Sandy Jr. (1908–1969) and Viola S. Frazier (1908–1975) and the granddaughter of Sandy Sr. (1880–1939) and Mary Chavis Frazier (1880–1960).

Eva told me:

Son, as a young girl growing up we lived next door to our grandmother's house. We used to call

Top: Joseph Deleston Sr. *Courtesy of Marie Deleston.*

Middle: Emily "Cord" Deleston. *Courtesy of Marie Deleston.*

Bottom: Eva Frazier Seabrook. *Family photograph.*

her Grim Ma. Our father and mother had fourteen children. Twelve of us were raised to adulthood. I was the seventh child. I remember from the age of five, when our father came home after a long day of working on the farm. He would perform many chores. I especially remember when he would get his hand saw and cut lumber, making us benches to sit on because there were no chairs, but he did not want us to sit on the floor. That was a happy time for us. I loved those benches so much. It was like someone gave me something I couldn't describe because it was made by my father.

Our family was poor. I remember my mother went to Leon's five-and-ten-cent store and brought all of us an aggie cup and pan to eat and drink out of instead of those pint jars we were accustomed to using. Although there were a lot of children, Mama would always cook enough food in case anyone else stopped by and wanted to eat.

I remember during the winter months after doing our homework and chores, Papa, Mama and all the children would sit around the chimney fireplace, and they would explain to us how to love one another, our extended family and others by giving and sharing what we had. Besides working on most of the farms on the island after school, my Papa and Mama had a small farm that we had to work on as well. Saturday seemed so special to us. This was when we helped to prepare our clothes for Sunday and for the week for school.

Eva continued:

Although we attended St. James Presbyterian Church's Sunday school in our community, there was this wonderful woman named Mrs. Oralee Brown. She had Sunday school every Sunday afternoon, and we went there also. When there were night services at the church, the parents and children would hold hands and walk to church in both hot and cold weather. It was not a short walk. It was a long walk, but we made it. When it rained, Papa would go down the road in the community and find one of the men with a car to take us where we needed to go. I remember working in the field on our parent's farm watching my brother plowing with the mule, and working so hard at a young age, but all of that made him an honest and successful man. Our parents raised us with morals and values and to treat people the way we wanted to be treated, but most of all to believe in and trust in God.

Ora Lee Brown

Ora Lee Brown. *Courtesy of McKever Brown Jr.*

Ora Lee Brown was born in 1919 and died in 2000. Her husband, McKever Brown, was born in 1914. Ora Lee was the daughter of Isabelle Whaley (1896) and Arthur Lee Chavos (1889), the granddaughter of Henry (1861) and Peggy S. Whaley (1864), and the great-granddaughter of slaves Daniel (1833) and Clarissa Whaley (1837). McKever was the son of Cuffy (1874) and his wife, Clara Brown (1877), and the grandson of slave Daniel Drown (1834–1915). The Whaleys and the Browns were farmers on the Grimball Plantation.

Ora Lee was a seamstress in the community. She sewed and made clothes for people on James Island. She was a member of St. James Presbyterian Church on James Island and the second female to be appointed as elder in the 1950s under the leadership of the Reverend Marion A. Sanders. McKever served in the United States Navy during World War II. After his discharge, he bought a twelve-seat passenger bus that he used to help transport black farmers to the Charleston Market to sell their vegetables. He also transported black students to school in Charleston prior to the South Carolina Department of Education supplying buses to transport African Americans to school. McKever also owned a small farm and worked as a janitor for the W.G. Meggett High School on James Island until he retired. Ora Lee and McKever's eldest son, Gordon Brown, was inducted into the African American Golfer's Hall of Fame on May 29, 2005, in Fort Lauderdale, Florida. Many descendants of Ora Lee and McKever still live on James Island.

Omega Deleston

Omega Deleston was the daughter of Frank (1875–1956) and Annie Cromwell Deleston (1878–1948), the granddaughter of slaves Joseph (1838) and Dolly Frazier Deleston (1852), and the great-granddaughter of Frank (1810) and Rose Deleston (1815). Her parents, grandparents and great-grandparents are all buried at the Ever Green Cemetery on the Grimball Plantation. Omega's family were sharecroppers and farmers on the Grimball

Plantation, and like many young black women, the only job available to her during that time besides farm work was domestic work, which she did for many years.

Leon Deleston, Omega's eldest son, and I grew up together in the Grimball Road community and attended elementary and high schools together. We also ended up enlisting in the United States Army together. After his discharge from the United States Army, Leon migrated to New York. In addition to his work while in New York, Leon also became a preacher. He later returned to James Island and purchased a home after retiring from his job. Omega is buried at the St. James Presbyterian Church cemetery. Although many members of the Deleston family migrated north to seek a better life during the 1940s and 1950s, many remained on James Island.

Lillie Mae Chisolm

Lillie Mae Chisolm was born in 1917 and died in 1991. Her husband, Fred "Doug" Chisolm, was born in 1914 and died in 2002. Lillie Mae was the daughter of Isabelle Whaley (1896) and Arthur Lee Chavous (1889), the granddaughter of Henry (1861) and Peggy S. Whaley (1864), and the great-granddaughter of slaves Daniel (1833) and Clarissa Whaley (1837). Fred "Doug" Chisolm (1914) was the son of Fortune (1864) and Livinia Chisolm (1877–1944) and the grandson of John (1844) and Rosa Chisolm (1846).

Top: Omega Deleston. *Courtesy of Elaine William.*

Middle: Lillie Mae Chisolm. *Courtesy of Vivian Chisolm.*

Bottom: Fred "Doug" Chisolm. *Courtesy of Vivian Chisolm.*

The Chisolms and the Whaleys were farmers on the Grimball Plantation. Fred "Doug" Chisolm served in the United States Navy during World War II. After his discharge, he worked at the Charleston Naval Shipyard and retired after thirty-four years of service. He was a member of the First Baptist Church and chairman of the deacon board. He was considered one of the pillars in the community. Lillie Mae was a member and elder of the St. James Presbyterian Church. She was a housewife but also did some domestic work during those trying times on James Island. Many of their descendants still live on James Island.

Isabelle W. Chavos

Isabelle W. Chavos was born in 1896 and died in 1956. Her husband was Arthur L. Chavos (1889). Isabelle was the daughter of Henry (1861) and Peggy S. Whaley (1864) and the granddaughter of Daniel (1833) and Clarissa Whaley (1837). The Whaleys were farmers on the Grimball Plantation during the slavery, sharecropping and farming eras. Many descendants of Isabelle and Arthur Chavos still live on James Island.

Above, left: Hermina Garland (left), Isabelle W. Chavos (seated,) and Rosa Turner. *Courtesy of Vivian Chisolm.*

Above, right: Arthur L. Chavos and his baby brother. *Courtesy of Vivian Chisolm.*

Mattie Palmer Whaley

Mattie and Lorenzo Whaley. *Courtesy of Jacqueline W. Young.*

Mattie Palmer Whaley was born in 1917 and died in 2007. Her husband, Lorenzo Whaley, was born in 1916 and died in 1997. Mattie was the daughter of Hester Fell (1876) and Royal Palmer (1860–1935), and the granddaughter of slaves Elizabeth Fell (1842) and Amos Prioleau (1838). The Fell family were slaves on the Dill Plantation during the slavery and sharecropping eras.

Lorenzo was the grandson of Henry Whaley (1861) and the great-grandson of Daniel Whaley (1833). According to the archives of the Payne RUME Church on Camp Road, Daniel Whaley was one of the founding fathers under the leadership of Reverend Prince "Pappy" White (1830) in 1875. The Whaleys were slaves, sharecroppers and farmers on the Grimball Plantation.

Lorenzo was employed by H.W. Halter and Son Meat Company for many years. He was later employed by Emanuel-El Synagogue in Charleston until he retired. I remember Lorenzo as a quiet, easygoing person who would greet everyone with a smile and a "how you doing." He was a generous man who shared the meat that he bought from his employer with the poor in the community. Lorenzo and Mattie were lifelong members of the St. James Presbyterian Church. Mattie was also an elder, deacon and division leader. Many descendants of the Whaleys and Fells still live on James Island.

Robert "Robbie" Gilliard Jr.

Robert "Robbie" Gilliard Jr. was born in 1915. His wife, Melvina "Blossom" Champagne, was born in 1918. Robert Jr. was the son of Robert Sr. (1893) and Irene Chavis Gilliard (1895–1949), the grandson of slaves Paul (1841) and Betsy Matthew Chavis (1850) and the great-grandson of Cudjo (1813) and Mary Chavis (1819). They were sharecroppers and farmers on the Grimball Plantation. Cudjo and his wife came to James Island by way of

Robert "Robbie" Gilliard. *Courtesy of Julia A. Frazier.*

Elloree, South Carolina, from Sierra Leone. Many descendants of Cudjo and Mary Chavis still live on the property they bought from the Grimballs during the sharecropping and farming eras.

Blossom was the daughter of Richard "Manny" (1889–1936) and Virginia "Mama" Brown Champagne (1896–1963) and the granddaughter of slaves, Smiley (1845) and Grace Brown (1872). They were sharecroppers and farmers on the Dill Plantation. Robert and Blossom migrated north to New York during the 1940s. They married and raised their family there. I remember Robert and Blossom returning to James Island on many occasions to visit with relatives.

After their deaths, Robert and Blossom, his brother John and his sisters Elizabeth and Maybelle were all buried in New York. Many relatives of Robert and Blossom still live on James Island. I will always remember that day in 1949 when Robert's mother, my grandaunt, Irene Chavis Gilliard, died. While the family was gathered at her house comforting one another, we received word that her sister, Alice Chavis McNeal, had died on the Sol Legare Plantation.

Morris Smalls Sr.

Morris Smalls Sr. was born in 1916 and died in 1984. His wife, Vernell Cromwell Smalls, was born in 1919. Morris was the son of Isaac (1892) and Mary Simmons Smalls (1896) and the grandson of slaves, Hector (1846) and Elizabeth Smalls (1846).

Morris served in the U.S. Navy during World War II. After his discharge, he worked for the government as a pipe fitter at the Charleston Naval Shipyard. He became the first certified African American pipe-fitting instructor in the shipyard's history. He was a member of the First Baptist Church on James Island. Many of Morris's relatives still live on James Island.

Morris Smalls Sr. *Courtesy of Berthel Smalls Ward.*

Abraham "Bram" Richardson

Abraham "Bram" Richardson was born in 1918 and died in 1991. He was married to Ruby Barron Richardson. Abraham was the son of Robert Jr. (1866) and Pauline W. Richardson (1888) and the grandson of Robert Sr. (1825) and Jane Richardson (1833). They were farmers on the Grimball Plantation.

Abraham, "Bram" or "Berlin," as he was affectionately called, served in the U.S. Army during World War II. While there, he was captured and became a prisoner of war (POW). The POW initials were branded on his arm during his confinement. After his discharge, he worked at the Charleston Naval Shipyard in North Charleston until he retired in 1979. During a conversation I had with Mari Richardson, Abraham's daughter, she said:

> *Frazier, as a young man, my father was known for his physical strength, natty attire and beautiful fast cars. He owned a convertible car in the 1940s. After enlisting in the army, my grandfather built a garage to house one of my fathers's prized vehicles until he returned home and would not permit anyone else to drive it.*

Abraham "Bram" Richardson. *Courtesy of Mari Richardson Bolden.*

> *My father's nickname of Berlin was given to him because he loved shopping at the upscale men's clothier in downtown Charleston, Berlin's Men's Wear.*

I also found out that Abraham was quite a boxer. Mari said:

> *Scheduled boxing matches were commonplace on the island, with Abram usually being the victor. He also boxed while in the army. He later married my mother, Ruby Barron, a beauty from Adams Run, South Carolina, in 1946. He often said that since everyone on the island was related, he thought it best that he marry a lady from elsewhere. The wedding almost did not take place due to the whims of Ruby's strict aunt, who raised*

her after the death of her mother. It was reported to her that Abram had visited Ruby without an appropriate chaperone or supervision, which was a dating requirement during that era.

He often joked that due to his being "a good catch," he had to bribe several former girlfriends who threatened to show up and disrupt the wedding. With Abram, however, one never knew if his stories were true or fictional. But his listeners waited in anticipation for his next tale. My father was an excellent provider and always took good care of his family. He stressed the importance of a good education and ensured that opportunities were made available for his children. He also stressed the importance of preserving the legacies of our forbears and respecting their hard work and commitment to make things better for their children. They did this in the form of land ownership. Abram believed strongly in paying property taxes "no matter what" and frequently paid taxes for family members who were unable or unwilling to pay.

After his retirement from the Charleston Naval Shipyard, my father continued to pursue his love of boating and fishing. He always owned at least two boats—one for fishing and one for racing. He excelled in both. He taught many younger men how to navigate the channels and waterways. He loved entertaining at backyard gatherings, where he displayed his keen sense of humor, zest for life and wisdom. His younger brother, George Richardson, who retired from the United State Marine Corp, proudly boasted, "Abram was a man among men."

I knew Abram and recalled that Abram, Morris Smalls and Thomas Backman were among the first group of African American males who owned new cars during the late 1940s and 1950s on James Island.

Robert Jr. and Pauline Richardson

Pauline W. Richardson was born in 1888. Her husband, Robert Richardson Jr., was born in 1866. Pauline was the daughter of Henry (1861) and Peggy S. Whaley (1864) and the granddaughter of Daniel (1833) and Clarissa Whaley (1837). Robert Jr. was the son of Robert Sr. (1825) and Jane Richardson (1833). Robert (1825) was one of the slaves who were given land on the McLeod Plantation by the Freedmen's Bureau after slavery. Robert and Pauline were farmers on the Grimball Plantation.

Left: Pauline W. Richardson with her children. *Courtesy of Mari Richardson Bolden.*

Below: Penn Station, New York, during the early 1930s. Robert Richardson Jr. (center) is standing in a light gray coat with his family, waiting to board a southbound train to Charleston after visiting with them in New York. *Courtesy of Mari Richardson Bolden.*

Louisa Prioleau Moore Young

Louisa Prioleau Moore Young. *Family photograph.*

Louisa Prioleau Moore Young was born in 1859. Her second husband was Moses Young (1862). Louisa was one of nine children born to James Prioleau (1823) and his wife, Betty Prioleau (1831). James Prioleau came to James Island from the St. Steven's area of Berkeley County. He settled on the Grimball Plantation, where he sharecropped for a period of time. He eventually became a farmer and began farming his own land. Over the years, he became a successful farmer who was able to purchase over one hundred acres of land from the Grimball Plantation.

According to church's minutes obtained from the white James Island Presbyterian Church located on Fort Johnson Road near Folly Road, between the years of 1833 and 1845, there were 153 slaves, 1 freed slave and 33 white members attending the white church prior to it being destroyed by fire in 1865. My research revealed that the only two listed freedmen on James Island during this period were James Prioleau and Simeon Pinckney of the Hinson Plantation. It is believed that James Prioleau was buried at the church's cemetery in the early years

Following his death, in a will dated 1889 James left his nine children equal shares of his property on Grimball Road, located on James Island and Taylor Island across the river from Mosquito Beach. Louisa once lived on her father's property on Taylor Island across the river from Sol Legare. The property that James Prioleau bought for his family is still owned by his descendants. Louisa was the great-grandmother of Francis Prioleau Frazier, my wife.

Joseph and Naomi Cromwell

Joseph Cromwell was born in 1908. His wife, Naomi Cromwell, was born in 1911. Joseph was the grandson of Louisa Prioleau (1859). Naomi was the daughter of John (1878) and Martha Chavis (1883), all from the Grimball Plantation.

Far left: Joseph Cromwell. *Courtesy of Hazel Cromwell Harley.*

Left: Naomi Cromwell. *Courtesy of Hazel Cromwell Harley.*

Joseph was known in the community by his nickname, "Joe." Although he had a small farm, Joe worked at the Charleston Naval Shipyard for many years. He was also a carpenter. Many of Joseph and Naomi's descendants still live on James Island.

John and Mary Prioleau

John Prioleau was born in 1897 and died in 1985. He was married to Mary Gilliard Prioleau (1899). John was the son of Thomas (1881) and Mary Prioleau (1881). John's family were farmers on the Grimball Plantation. He was a member of the St. James Presbyterian Church, where he served as an elder and clerk of session. He also served in the U.S. Army during World War I.

During one of my conversations with Mary Laurencin, the daughter of John and Mary, she said:

> *Frazier, our parents were God-fearing people who taught us to love and obey God as our heavenly father as well as them. They were loving and caring people. They believed in "not sparing the rod." They were from the old school, protective of their children, yet tolerating no disrespect from us.*
>
> *They taught us to be respectful to each other, to love, be kind as well, especially to older people in the community. They were churchgoing people, active in the church, and their children had to be active as well. We had chores to do, work in the field and home, along with doing our schoolwork. They*

Far left: John Prioleau. *Courtesy of Mary Laurencin.*

Left: Mary Gilliard Prioleau. *Courtesy of Mary Laurencin.*

> *believed in education. Never settle for less. We had to do our schoolwork by oil lamp. Our parents could not afford electricity. It wasn't easy, but we made it with their encouragement. Because of them and God, we are what we are today. Our accomplishments cover various fields: minister, teacher, medical technician, research scientist, chemical engineer and several other professions.*

Many of John and Mary's descendants still live on James Island.

Helen Richardson Prioleau

Helen Richardson Prioleau was born in 1915. Her husband, Benjamin Prioleau, was born in 1910. Helen was the granddaughter of Sam B. Richardson (1868). She was a member of and an elder in the St. James Presbyterian Church.

Several of Helen's daughters migrated to New York from the 1950s through the 1970s in search of a better life during those trying times in the South. Although two of her daughters live in New York, they remain loyal to their beloved James Island and visit relatives regularly.

The following excerpt is from a conversation and a letter that I obtained from Helen's daughter, Alice R. Brooks:

> *Frazier, my mother inspired me to be who I am today. Among the countless things that my mother taught me was, first, how to pray for wisdom,*

Helen Richardson Prioleau.
Family photograph.

knowledge and understanding so that I would grow to be an independent young woman, capable of taking care of myself. She then taught me to always have respect for my elders. Without her teachings, I don't know where I would be today.

Another daughter, Elizabeth P. Lee, said:

Frazier, I have been inspired by my mother. I have truly learned to trust in the Lord Jesus Christ. Many times I heard her say, "Jesus is my only friend." In difficult times, she would call on the Lord. The Lord would hear her cry and answer her prayers. I thank God for my parents, Helen and Benjamin Prioleau. I am who I am because of them.

In a note, another daughter, Julia R. Quarles, said, "Frazier, my mother was an extraordinary, exceptional woman who taught me the ways of life that I later passed on to my children." Another daughter, Gwendolyn R. Johnson, said, "Frazier, Mama never complained about life, even though situations and circumstances sometimes became very challenging. She would say, 'Life is good, always try to do the best you can and treat people right. Be able to raise your hands and say, Lord Have Mercy.'"

Still another daughter, Catherine P. Capestany, said:

> *Frazier, my mother Helen deeply inspired me through constant guidance, vigilance and love. Next to the Blessed Mother Mary, she was the sweetest, dearest mother ever. She was my role model, my confidante and my best friend. She taught me how to love my family, to be humble, obedient and faithful and true to myself and to God and my Savior, Jesus Christ. Lastly, she taught me to be a woman in my own right. I shall be eternally grateful to God for giving me my beautiful mother. I deeply miss her presence among us. May her soul continue to rest in peace.*

Lastly, in a letter and a phone conversation with me, Naomi P. Gilliard said:

> *Frazier, I remember my mother's quiet, reassuring and comforting manner when I shared something with her that was painful for me. She would always reassure me that everything would be all right. Just pray and trust in God. She was a wonderful mother, with a good sense of humor. She was a lady, a wife, a mother, homemaker, seamstress, beautician and a trusting and loyal friend. She instilled good moral standards in us. They insisted that we get a good education and saw to it that we did. My parents also taught us to respect each other from the eldest to the youngest.*
>
> *The most precious gift my mother ever gave me was she shared Jesus Christ. In our house, he was God. There was no other God but him. I'm reminded of my mother's illness that led to her passing. We, her children, got together and held a pray service for her. We all gathered around her bed and began to share with her our feelings. I told my mother how much I loved her and that even though daddy was gone that we loved him also and that they were good parents and that we thank God for them.*

Many of Helen and Ben's descendants still live on James Island and throughout the metropolitan area.

Janie Middleton Moore

Janie Middleton Moore. *Family photograph.*

Janie Middleton Moore was born in 1895. Her husband, Oswald Moore, was born in 1882. Oswald was the son of Reese (1868) and Syla Moore (1870). Janie was the daughter of Remus (1856) and Wilhmenia Forest Middleton. They were all farmers on the Grimball Plantation.

In a statement from her daughter, Florence M. Chisolm, Florence said:

> *Life growing up with Papa and Mama was good. There were eleven children in the family, and Mama raised eight of them to adulthood. Papa was a farmer, and all of the children worked in the field. Mama had a roadside fruit and vegetable stand on the corner of Grimball and Folly Road. Papa was very strong in discipline. Mama didn't discipline, but they were both on one accord. If you asked one, you had to ask the other. If one said no, the other said no. If one said yes, the other said yes. They never allowed us to play one parent against the other.*

In a conversation with her grandson, Reverend Leonard E. Moore Sr., he said:

> *Granddaddy was a strict disciplinarian. He believed in hard work. He believed that a man should take care of his family. He did all the shopping and paid all the bills. Grandmamma raised the children and kept the house. Papa was one of the first black farmers on James Island. He would take his crops to the Farmers Market in downtown Charleston. Mama had a fruit and vegetables stand. Both were strong believers of the church. Ossie and the boys were raised as Baptist and attended First Baptist Church, while Janie and the girls were raised as Presbyterians and attended St. James Presbyterian Church. Both were hard workers.*

In conversations with Adrienne "Peachey" Chisolm Cox, she said:

> *Frazier, when I came along, my grandmother was older. My grandfather had passed away so I never knew him. However, I heard many stories. I do remember going to the vegetable stand to help my grandmother. I would*

also sit on the porch with her and shell beans. She always told me to have manners because manners would take you much further than money. She would also quote her favorite scriptures, Hebrews 11 and Psalms 121. I have adopted them as my favorites, too. I can really say that my grandmother loved her church, and she loved her pastor, the late Reverend C.L. Campbell Jr. She attended church every Sunday until she couldn't. She always offered whatever she had, even if it was just a little.

Many of Oswald and Janie Moore's descendants still live on James Island.

Dorothy Brown Thomas

Dorothy Brown Thomas. *Courtesy of Dorothy Brown Thomas.*

Dorothy Brown Thomas was born in 1921. Her husband, George Thomas, was born in 1920. Dorothy was the daughter of Josiah (1870) and Clohie "Carrie" Brown (1881–1965). They were farmers on the Grimball Plantation. Dorothy was born and raised on the Grimball Plantation. After she married George, they moved to the city of Charleston. Many of Dorothy's descendants still live on James Island.

John Roper Sr.

John Roper Sr. *Courtesy of William Roper.*

John Roper Sr. was born in 1908. He was married to Ernestine Lafayette Roper (1912). John was the son of Christopher (1886) and Diane Roper (1889). Ernestine was the daughter of William (1885) and Maria Lafayette (1882). The Ropers were farmers on the Seabrook Plantation, and the Lafayettes were farmers on the Sol Legare Plantation.

John graduated from Avery Institute in Charleston in 1931. He taught many World War II veterans the fine art of agriculture. Mr. Roper was also a Sunday school teacher at the St. James Presbyterian Church. I was one of his students during his tenure as teacher.

He was among the first black men hired by the United States Post Office in Charleston, if not the first, and was considered a pioneer in the profession by African Americans on James Island. I believed as a teenager, and still do today, that one of John Roper's greatest attributes was how he mastered the English language. Many of John and Ernestine's descendants still live on James Island.

David "Dave" and Harriet Richardson

Harriet Richardson. *Courtesy of Edna "Mattie" Richardson.*

David "Dave" Richardson was born in 1905. He was married to Harriet Richardson (1908). Harriet was the daughter of Elizabeth "Lizzie" (1888) and Easton Robinson (1887) and the granddaughter of slaves Phillip (1850) and Harriet Robinson (1850).

I knew Dave personally. He was considered by many James Islanders to be an entrepreneur skilled in many different areas. He was a carpenter, businessman and the first and only African American to own and operate a dry cleaning business on James Island. It was once located on Folly Road across from James Prioleau Road. He also owned and operated a business called Curvene Piccolo Joint (nightclub) near that same location. Additionally, he was the owner and operator of a fish and shrimp trawler during the earlier years. Many of Dave and Harriet's family still live on James Island.

Henry W. Halter

Henry W. Halter and his wife, Annie Jewell Halter, were the owners of Halter and Son Pantry Store, once located at the intersection of Folly and Grimball Roads. It was destroyed by fire in 1943.

Henry was the father of Herman W. Halter Sr., the grandfather of Herman Halter Jr. and the great-grandfather of Herman W. Halter IV. During the 1900s, when James Island was considered a wilderness composed of primarily woods, farmland, dirt roads and trails, the only paved road on the island was Folly Road, a two-lane highway that ran from Charleston to Folly Beach.

Henry Halter built and owned the Pantry Store at the corner of Folly and Grimball Road. The store was patronized by both black and white people from the Grimball and Seabrook Plantations, as well as other neighboring plantations on James Island. The store was a favorite stop for motorists traveling from Charleston to Folly Beach. During that time, the store was one of three on James Island that sold everything from rice, grits, fatback, butts meat, molasses, pig feet, chicken feet and every kind of food item that was a necessity for the household. It also sold nails, roofing paper and other items needed for household repairs. When I was ten years old, my father would send me on a shortcut behind our house, through the field and woods, to Halter and Son Pantry Store to buy food for the family.

In a phone conversation supported by a letter in April 2008, Lizetta, wife of Herman Halter and daughter-in-law of Henry, said:

> *Frazier around the last part of January or the first of February 1943, the store burned down and the only thing left standing was the sign for the store that identified it as H.W. Halter & Son Pantry Store. I recall after the fire all the black people that credited from the store during the*

From left to right: Tommy A. Halter in his navy uniform; Tommy's mother, Mary Stoke Halter; Annie Jewell Halter; and Annie's husband, Henry W. Halter. *Courtesy of Lizetta R. Halter.*

Left: Lizetta Halter. *Courtesy of Lizetta R. Halter.*

Below: The Halter and Son Pantry Store at the intersection of Grimball and Folly Roads, along with Halter's two houses to the left of the store and one across Folly Road. It also depicts the James Island landscape during the 1940s. This photo was taken by William Scott, manager of Carolina Skyways Airport located on Riverland Drive. *Courtesy of Lizetta R. Halter.*

week and paid on Saturday came and paid Mr. Halter every penny they owed him, even though the book that kept the record was burned during the fire. They pleaded with him to rebuild the store. In June 1943, Mr. Henry rebuilt the store, and his daughter, Margie Womack, was married in the store prior to the reopening.

Margie Halter Womack and I worked in the store all day during World War II. Herman, my husband, was in France and Germany, and Alvin was in the Pacific. Mr. Henry would open the store at six o'clock in the morning so the people could get their lunch before they went in the fields to work. Margie and I would go to work at 8:00 a.m. and work until closing time. Frazier, I will be eighty-two in July.

Many of Henry W. Halter's descendants still live on James Island.

Edna "Mattie" R. Richardson

Edna "Mattie" R. Richardson was born in 1915. She was married to John Richardson (1910). Edna was the granddaughter of slaves Peter (1840) and Leia Simmons Brown (1856). John Richardson was the grandson of John (1848) and Emma Richardson (1841). Peter Brown was listed as one of the founding fathers of Payne RMUE Church, Camp Road, under the leadership of Reverend Prince "Pappy" White (1830) in 1875.

During interviews with Edna over the past several years, she told me:

Frazier, from the time I was a little girl visiting my Grandma Leia on the Rivers Plantation, she told me and other family members that she and several other slaves walked to Charleston from a place far away and were sold to the Rivers Plantation.

My research revealed that my great-grandfather, Jake "Jacob" Smalls, was with Edna's grandmother, Leia, and the group of slaves who walked from South Santee in McClellanville, South Carolina, to the Old Slave Market on Chalmers Street in Charleston, where they were sold to their respective plantation owners on James Island.

In a conversation with Harriet R. Bright, the daughter of Edna, she said:

Frazier, back in the days of the 1950s and the 1960s, our parents provided us with nourishing moral standards and a well-balanced life growing up.

Edna "Mattie" Richardson. *Family photograph.*

We felt the security of having both parents at home after their working hours. There were seven siblings in our family, but each one of us was unique in our own way. Dad was a very strict and timely father. We had time for leisure as well as chores before bedtime. I remember the days when Dad allowed us five minutes to talk on the telephone. Television was turned off at 10:00 p.m. We were in bed no later than 11:00 p.m. We were out of bed by 7:00 a.m. The bedroom was cleaned and beds made by 8:00 a.m. Mom liked to set up two ironing boards on Saturday.

Harriet continued:

Mom would put all the siblings' clothes into a bundle of two tied-up tablecloths. The girls had to iron until all siblings' clothes were ironed and put away before we could have any kind of outdoor outing. We were not allowed to go anywhere if we didn't go to church on Sunday. Our

> *games were monitored on Saturday because on Sunday we had to go to church. We could not play games like card games, dice games, checker games or any sort of games that reminded Dad of gambling. Our parents' teachings and believing in God, and their spiritual and moral values, are the reasons we are blessed and will continue to thank God and our parents, John and Edna.*

Many of John and Edna's descendants still live on James Island.

SEABROOK PLANTATION

SLAVES AND THEIR DESCENDANTS

Aida White Moore

Aida White Moore. *Family photograph.*

Aida White Moore was born in 1914 and died in 2005. She was married to the Reverend John H. Moore (1914). Aida was the daughter of slaves Middleton (1854) and Elizabeth Brown White (1878) and the granddaughter of slave Prince "Pappy" White (1830). Pappy was the overseer on Seabrook Plantation during the slavery and sharecropping eras.

Between 2001 and her death in 2005, I interviewed Aida on several occasions. During one of those conversations, she said:

Frazier, I was born and raised on the Seabrook Plantation, where my daddy and granddaddy were slaves. My daddy told me that Mr. Seabrook, the owner of the plantation, was killed during the Confederate War. He said Mrs. Seabrook went to the Slave Market in Charleston and bought my granddaddy, Prince "Pappy" White, and made him the overseer on the plantation. My granddaddy was Payne Church's first preacher after the building was completed in 1875.

Aida was a lifelong member of and historian for Payne RMUE Church on Camp Road. Many of Aida's descendants still live on James Island.

Samuel C. Gilliard

Samuel C. Gilliard. *Courtesy of Wilburn Gilliard.*

Samuel C. Gilliard was born in 1919. He was married to Elouise Gilliard (1923–2004). Sam was the son of Alexander (1893) and Elizabeth Gilliard (1900) and the grandson of George (1873) and Laura Gilliard (1873–1947). Sam and Elouise had one son, Wilburn Gilliard, and a daughter, Emma Gilliard.

During a conversation with Wilburn, he said:

Frazier, my father was known and affectionately called Sam by the people in the community. He retired from one of the local shipyards repairing and caulking ships. Before that he worked as a carpenter, plumber's helper, electrician and a number of other things while farming on the side.

Sam was well known and had a number of sayings to explain who he was or something about him. He became bald in his early twenties and was often made fun of. Folk would say that he looked like a preacher because of his baldness. He would often reply, "Grass don't grow on busy streets, and it sure can't grow on concrete." In reference to the type of work he did, he would say that he was a "jack of all trades and a master of none."

Wilburn continued:

My grandfather, Alexander, did various odd jobs to support his family but was primarily a farmer and fisherman. He plowed for the Seabrooks, the owners of the Seabrook Plantation in Secessionville. My grandfather was fond of me. We lived next door to him. His pet name for me was

"Pompey." He did special things for me to show his grandfatherly love. He was a member of First Baptist Church and served as a deacon until his early death of cancer.

Many of Alexander and Elizabeth's descendants still live on James Island.

Betsy Smalls Campbell

Betsy Smalls Campbell was born in 1898. She was married to Joseph Campbell (1897). Betsy was the daughter of Henry (1838) and Clorie Smalls. Joseph was the son of Tony (1855) and Nellie Campbell (1862). The Campbells were slaves and farmers on the Seabrook Plantation. The Smalls were slaves and farmers on the Dill Plantation.

The family stated that according to oral history reports from family members and descendants, Betsy was an Indian from the Cherokee Tribe. As a young teenager, I knew Ms. Betsy, and her features strongly resembled those of Indian ancestry. During a conversation with Nellie Moultrie Clark, Betsy's granddaughter, Nellie said:

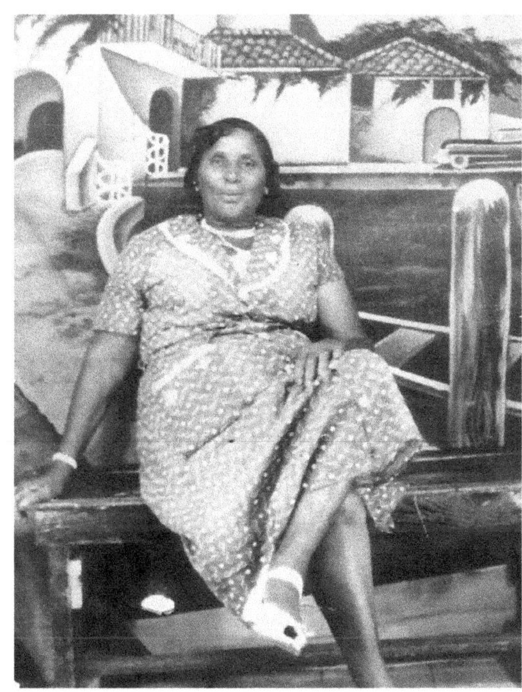

Betsy Smalls Campbell. *Courtesy of Nellie Clark.*

Frazier, my grandmother and grandfather were married in 1920. They had nine sons and three daughters. She was a housewife, seamstress and farmer. Her farm yielded such crops as tomatoes, okra, beans, peanuts and sweet and white potatoes. She would have one of the men in the community who owned a car or truck drive her to the Market on Meeting Street in Charleston to sell her vegetables. During the last twelve years of his life, her husband, Joseph, was bedridden. My grandmother took care of his every need until his passing.

As a young girl, I remember hearing her telling my mom, Nellie, that whenever she died to make sure her feet were clean. I was a little girl then and didn't understand why she said that. But as time went on, I can understand what she meant. She worked so hard that she didn't have time to give herself a bath. But, through all this, she was a jolly lady and the grandchildren and neighbors love her. Frazier, those are some of things I remember and love about my grandmother.

Many of Betsy and Joseph Campbell's descendants still live on James Island.

Henry "Dad" Singelton

Henry "Dad" Singelton. *Family photograph.*

Henry "Dad" Singelton was born in 1925 and died in 2005. He was married to Evelyn Brown Singelton (1927). Henry was the son of William (1890) and Roxanna Singelton (1892) and the grandson of Louis (1846) and Sarah Singelton (1856). Evelyn was the daughter of Abraham "Humble" (1885) and Estelle Brown and the granddaughter of Daniel Brown (1834–1915).

Henry was affectionately called "Dad" by the people in the community. He was one of the original fifty-six men who founded the Sons of Elijah Masonic Lodge #457 on James Island. He was a member of the St. James Presbyterian Church on James Island. Evelyn was a member of the Church of Christ. In a conversation with Lucille S. Gilliard, Henry's daughter, she said:

Frazier, there were nine children in our family. My father worked on a shrimp boat and dock on Folly Beach. Later, he got a job at Denton's Shipyard and worked there until he retired. While he worked at the shipyard to help supplement his income, he had a small vegetable farm near our house. All of the children helped plant the seeds and harvest the vegetables to sell at the Market in Charleston.

Among the many words of wisdom my father had for us, his favorite was, "As long as you live in this world, have respect for your elders, and don't raise your hand higher than it can go." My father was a good man and left a lasting impression on me, and I will always think of his words of wisdom to us.

Many of Henry and Evelyn's descendants still live on James Island.

Anna Smith Seabrook

Anna Smith Seabrook was born in 1916. She was married to George "Joshie" Seabrook (1916). Anna was the daughter of Nathaniel (1888) and Eliza Smith (1890). George (1919) was the son of William (1879) and Catherine Seabrook (1885). Anna was born and raised on the Cut Bridge Section of the Dill Plantation. George was born and raised on the Seabrook Plantation. After Anna married George, they moved to the Peas Hill Section on the Seabrook Plantation, where they were farmers.

Anna Smith Seabrook. *Courtesy of James Middleton.*

In a statement, Anna's daughter said:

Frazier, in addition to working on the farms, our mother was a domestic worker. She liked to bake corn bread, macaroni and cheese and especially bake biscuits on Sunday. I remember waking up on Sunday morning to the aroma and smelling the gravy as she cooked the liver, grits and sweet potatoes for us. She would make sure we got up in the morning and get us ready for school. I remember being pregnant with my firstborn, and I couldn't stand the smell of liver and gravy. However, after getting myself together, I would be the first to sit at the table to eat that liver and grits.

> *Anna, our mother, grand- and great-grandmother, was a kind and religious women. She was a member of St. James Presbyterian Church and served on the floral committee. She was also a member of Alpha Tent #212 and a volunteer worker at the VA Hospital. The last two decades she lived at the AME Apartment on Fleming Road, where she was a mother figure to all that lived there.*

I recall Mrs. Anna as a very quiet and loving person who always greeted you with a smile and asked how your mother was doing. I went to St. James Parochial School with two of the Seabrook children—Mamie and George Jr. Many of Anna and George's descendants still live on James Island.

Mikell "Mike" and Lazarus Fludd

Mikell "Mike" Fludd was born in 1920. He was married to Ernestine Smalls Fludd. Mikell was the son of Edward "Eddie" (1892) and Betsy Fludd (1894), the grandson of slaves Lazarus (1850) and Hester Fludd

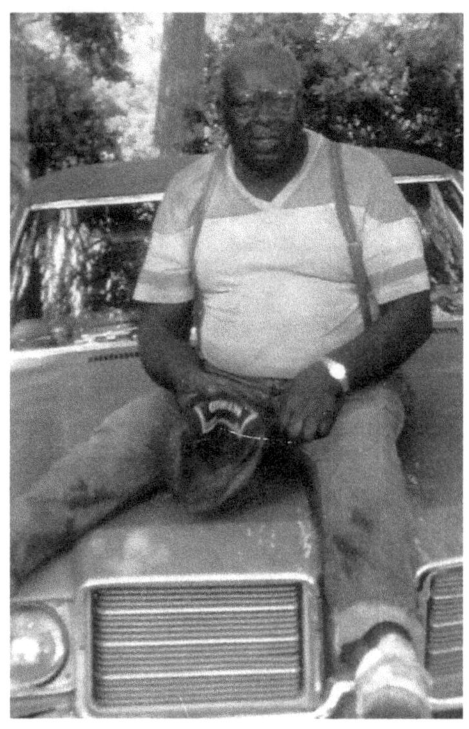

Mikell "Mike" Fludd. *Courtesy of Gerald Fludd.*

(1852) and the great-grandson of slave Molly Fludd (1830). Ernestine was the daughter of Alfred (1894) and Rosa Gladden Smalls, and the great-granddaughter of slaves Jacob "Jake" (1798) and Violet Smalls (1810). "Mike," as he was affectionately called, and his family lived in the Peas Hill area on James Island off Secessionville Road. They were farmers on the Seabrook Plantation.

Lazarus Fludd was one of several former slaves who helped carry lumber on his shoulders from the Seabrooks' boat landing at Wappoo Creek, down a trail approximately two and a half miles to the corner of Fort Johnson and Secessionville Roads. This location is where the first black St. James Presbyterian Church was built under the leadership of Reverend H.H. Hunter. It was completed in 1868. Fludd was one of the founding fathers of the church. Many of Lazarus Fludd's descendants still live on James Island.

Rosa Deleston Moultrie

Rosa Deleston Moultrie was born in 1895. She was married to Henry Moultrie (1898). Rosa was the daughter of Pricilla Deleston (1876), the

Rosa Deleston Moultrie surrounded by her six sons (left to right), John (1921), Franklin (1925), Henry Jr. (1927), William (1929), Ben (1930) and Arthur Lee (1933), and three daughters, Lilly (1923), Patsy (1924) and Mary J. (1927). Her son March (1919) was not present *Courtesy of William Moultrie.*

granddaughter of slaves Joseph (1838) and Dolly Frazier Deleston (1838), and the great-granddaughter of Frank (1810) and Rose Deleston (1815). All were slaves, sharecroppers and farmers on the Grimball Plantation and are buried in the Ever Green Slave Cemetery. Henry was the son of Frank (1855) and Lizzie Moultrie (1855). They were slaves, sharecroppers and farmers on the Grimball and Seabrook Plantations.

Many of Henry and Rosa Moultrie's descendants still live on James Island.

Sol Legare Plantation

Slaves and Their Descendants

Carrie Richardson

Carrie Richardson. *Courtesy of Edna "Mattie" Richardson.*

Carrie Richardson was born in 1893. Her husband, James Richardson, was born in 1890. James was the son of slaves, John (1848) and Emma Richardson (1841). James, like many other men during that time, was a farmer. He supported his family from the fruits of the land and the bounty he acquired from the river. Records reveal that James was drafted in the U.S. Army in 1918, and fought during World War I. Carrie was a housewife and also helped her husband with the farm. Many of James and Carrie Richardson's descendants still live on James Island.

Toby Singelton

Toby Singelton was born in 1910. He was married to Wilhelmina Chavis Singelton (1911). Toby was the son of Edward (1882) and Catherine

Singelton (1887). He was a member and elder of the St. James Presbyterian Church and was considered one of the pillars in the community. Toby was one of the original fifty-six men who helped organize the Sons of Elijah Lodge #457 on James Island and was one of its past masters.

During my conversations with George Singelton, Toby's son, over the years, George said:

Toby Singelton. *Family photograph.*

> *Son, let me tell you as a child how I grew up living with Toby and Wilhelmina. They were religious people. Toby was an elder, and Wilhelmina was a deacon at St. James Presbyterian Church. They were two people who worked and loved to worship together. They always put God before them in all that they did. Toby was a butler and a farmer. He proved to be a man that anyone could trust his word. Here was a man with very little education and a God-fearing person that could preach and pray on or about any occasion. I still follow his example and leadership knowing that Toby not only "talked the talk," but also walked the walk. From working in the field harvesting vegetables to his job as a butler, my father was a man of principle.*

Many of Toby and Wilhelmina Singelton's descendants still live in the Sol Legare area of James Island.

Rebecca Gilliard Wilder

Rebecca Gilliard Wilder was born in 1912 and died in 2007. She was married to Harrison Wilder (1907). Rebecca was the daughter of Lawrence (1887) and Margaret Singelton Gilliard (1895). Harrison was the son of Andrew (1876) and Mary Wilder (1881), the grandson of William (1865) and Sally (1885), and the great-grandson of slaves Harrison (1849) and Patient Matthew Wilder (1845).

Rebecca was raised on her parents' farm on the Sol Legare Plantation. Like many of the young people her age, she worked on the farms during the time

when the country was in a depression, and she worked to help the family. Rebecca was a member of and an elder in the St. James Presbyterian Church and a community activist in several organizations on James Island. Some of those organizations include the James Island Improvement Organization. She was also a committee member involved in organizing the first Town of James Island, Alpha Tent #212, and the Daughters of Elijah Order of the Eastern Star, Chapter #337.

Calvin and Mamie Chavis

Calvin Chavis was born in 1918. He was married to Mamie R. Chavis. Calvin was the son of Joseph (1888) and Maryann Chavis (1889). Mamie was the daughter of Benjamin "Dimmy" (1896) and Emma Jane Richardson (1898). She was also the granddaughter of George (1878) and Heita Richardson (1876).

They were farmers on the Sol Legare Plantation. After his marriage to Mamie, Calvin was drafted into the United States Army during World War II. Following his discharge from the army, Calvin worked as a long-distance truck driver. In addition to farming, Calvin and Mamie were members of the St. James Presbyterian Church. Mamie continues to serve as an elder and division leader. Calvin served as an usher during his lifetime. Many of Calvin and Mamie's descendants still live on James Island.

Top: Rebecca Gilliard Wilder. *Family photograph.*

Middle: Calvin Chavis. *Courtesy of Mamie Chavis.*

Bottom: Mamie R. Chavis. *Courtesy of Mamie Chavis.*

Andrew "Apple" Jr. and Laura Wilder

Andrew "Apple" Wilder Jr. was born in 1915. He was married to Laura Singelton Wilder (1922). Apple was the son of Andrew Sr. (1876) and Mary Wilder (1881). Laura was the daughter of Edward (1882) and Catherine Singelton (1887).

Apple and Laura operated the Board Walk Club. The club was located on Sol Legare Road at a place locally and nationally known as Mosquito Beach. They built the club over the water and marsh. The first section of the building was open, but the second was enclosed. Both sections had a dance floor and were located across the road from each other. This was one of three places that African Americans frequented. The others were Riverside Beach in Mount Pleasant and Fraser Beach on Johns Island. Between the years 1920 and 1970, segregation of the races was strictly enforced, and blacks were not allowed to go to Folly Beach or the Isles of Palms Beach.

I recall men and women dancing the Charleston and shagging during the late 1930s through the late 1940s. These are the same dances that people in Charleston now call beach music and the Shaggs.

Above, left: Andrew "Apple" Wilder Jr. *Courtesy of Alethia Singelton.*

Above, right: Laura Singelton Wilder. *Courtesy of Alethia Singelton.*

Mosquito Beach was formed out of a necessity. From the 1920s through the 1950s, African Americans had no public places on James Island to socialize or gather for any type of recreation. Several black men on James Island decided to start a business on property that their ancestors owned. This would be the beginning of Mosquito Beach.

These businesses were called juke joints and piccolo joints. Some of the men operating these businesses were Jack Walker, Erwin Singelton, James Lafayette, William "Bubba" Chavis, Sandy Brown, John "Cane" Chavis, Dave Backman, Richard Smalls and Andrew "Apple" Wilder, among others.

Harold "Yankee" and Ethelyn Singelton

Harold "Yankee" Singelton was born in 1920 and died in 2005. He was married to Ethelyn Singelton (1923). Harold was the son of Abraham (1897) and his wife, Mary Singelton (1901). Ethelyn was the daughter of Edward (1882) and his wife, Catherine Richardson Singelton (1887), and the granddaughter of Louis (1846) and Sarah Singelton (1856).

Harold served in the U.S. Army during World War II and was honorably discharged in 1942. Like many men from Sol Legare, he once owned an oyster house business. He was later employed by the Charleston Naval Shipyard for twenty-eight years before he retired. Harold was a

Left: Harold Singelton. *Courtesy of Ethelyn Singelton.*

Above: Ethelyn Singelton. *Courtesy of Ethelyn Singelton.*

member of St. James Presbyterian Church and one of the original fifty-six founders of the Sons of Elijah Masonic Lodge #457 on James Island. Many of Harold and Ethelyn Singelton's descendants still live in the Sol Legare section of James Island.

Joseph and Maryann Chavis

Joseph Chavis was born in 1888. He was married to Maryann Middleton Chavis (1889). Joseph was the son of slaves, Paul (1841–1925) and Betsy Chavis (1850). Maryann was the daughter of Remus Middleton (1856). They were farmers on the Grimball Plantation. Joseph married Maryann and moved to the Sol Legare Plantation, where they became farmers.

As a young boy, I recall everyone in the community referring to Maryann as "Cousin and Aunt Maryann." She was very friendly and sociable. Maryann's husband, Joseph, and my grandmother, Mary Chavis Frazier, were brother and sister. I remember during the 1940s through 1960s, Maryann would visit my grandmother on numerous occasions on the Grimball Plantation. Their conversations ranged from the Bible to the history of African Americans on

Above, left: Maryann Middleton Chavis. *Courtesy of Mamie Chavis.*

Above, right: Joseph Chavis preparing his mule to cultivate his farm on the Sol Legare Plantation. *Courtesy of Mamie Chavis.*

the island and what was needed to improve our neighborhood. If someone in the community wanted to know who their relatives were and did not have the knowledge and resources to do the research, they would go to Aunt Maryann. I fondly remember before she died giving her a ride home from my grandmother's house in a police cruiser. She said, "Son, you sure make me proud. We have a black man on James Island who is a policeman." Many of Joseph and Maryann's descendants still live on Sol Legare and other locations on James Island.

Jack and Diana Walker

Jack Walker was born in 1911. He was married to Diana Grant Walker (1913). Jack was the son of Perry Walker (1887) and Bertie Brown (1892), the grandson of Ben (1870) and Susan Brown (1875) and the great-grandson of Guy (1863) and Betty Walker (1864). Dianna was the daughter of James and Sarah Grant from Johns Island.

Like many men from the Sol Legare area, Jack fed his family with produce from the farm. He also supplemented their food supply by fishing,

Jack and Diana Walker. *Courtesy of Ann Walker Rivers.*

picking up oysters and crabbing. Jack was also an entrepreneur. He was one of the men on James Island who operated a piccolo joint on Mosquito Beach on Sol Legare Road. Many of Jack and Diana's children still live on James Island.

Henry Wallace

Henry Wallace. *Courtesy Levola Whaley.*

Henry Wallace was born in 1896. He was married to Rebecca Wallace (1893). Henry was the son of Benjamin (1875) and Hattie Wallace (1879), the grandson of slaves Crawford (1835) and Sophie Wallace (1850) and a descendant of Sarah Wallace (1781).

During a conversation with Levola W. Whaley, Henry's daughter, she said:

> *Frazier, my father was a man of compassion, caring, respect and love for his children and his neighbors in the Sol Legare Community. He was a hard worker and a dedicated father that reared six children after the death of our mother, Rebecca Wallace. He accomplished this with the help of a dedicated sister, Harriett Wallace, a loving and caring niece, Irene Wallace Wilder, and love from other family members.*
>
> *My father was a fisherman. He also had a small farm that taught his children the importance of working, going to school and getting an education. Sometimes we will tell him we don't have anything in the house to cook, and he would ask, "Do you have any rice?" We would say yes, and then he would tell us cook some rice until I get back. When he returned, he would bring a large bucket of shrimp and Mullet fish, or oysters. We were never hungry. He taught us to trust in the Lord with all our hearts and lean not on our own understanding. All you have to do is to acknowledge him and he will direct your path.*

Many of Rebecca and Henry's descendants still live on Sol Legare and in the James Island area.

George and Genevieve Lafayette

George Lafayette was born in 1919 and died in 2003. He was married to Genevieve Cromwell Lafayette. George was the son of William (1885) and Maria Lafayette (1882), the grandson of slaves James (1834) and Martha Lafayette (1847) and the great-grandson of Frank Lafayette (1800). The Lafayettes were farmers on the Legare Plantation.

Genevieve was the daughter of Richard (1884) and Wilhmenia Cromwell (1890) and the granddaughter of slaves Richard (1853) and Phoebe Cromwell (1854). The Cromwells were farmers on the Grimball Plantation.

George served in the U.S. Army during World War II. After his discharge from the army, he worked at the Charleston Naval Shipyard until he retired. George was one of the original fifty-six men who helped organize the Sons of Elijah Lodge on James Island. He was a member of the St. James Presbyterian Church and served on the trustee board for several years. Many Lafayette descendants still live on James Island.

Above: George Lafayette. *Courtesy of Genevieve Lafayette.*

Left: Genevieve Cromwell Lafayette. *Courtesy of Genevieve Lafayette.*

Wilhelmina Jackson

Wilhelmina Jackson. *Courtesy of Wilhelmina Jackson.*

Wilhelmina Jackson was born in 1921. She was the daughter of Wilson (1900) and Susan Jackson (1904), the granddaughter of Louis (1876) and Isabella Jackson (1880), the great-granddaughter of slave Plenty Jackson (1860) and the descendant of Cicero Sr. (1831), Charlotte (1844) and Henry Jackson (1818). Henry was one of the oldest slaves on James Island at the time of his death.

Wilhelmina is a member of the St. James Presbyterian Church on James Island and serves on the usher board. Many descendants of the Jacksons still live in the Sol Legare area of James Island.

Susie Brown Backman

Susie Brown Backman. *Courtesy of Thomas Backman Jr.*

Susie Brown Backman was born in 1922 and died in 1990. She was married to Thomas Backman (1919–1964). Thomas was the grandson of slaves Primus (1840) and Mary Backman (1842). Thomas started his fishing career as a teenager in 1940. The young entrepreneur married Susie, and she joined him as a fisherman. Beginning in 1944, they fished in the Stono River and the Sol Legare area with a small boat.

In 1952, after the purchase of a small shrimp trawler, the *Porkey*, Thomas and Susie went into business for themselves. The business began to prosper, and they opened Backman Seafood Company on Sol Legare Road, James Island, adjacent to the Sol Legare Creek.

Thomas died in 1964. After his death, Susie took over, and the business continued to thrive. Susie was a hard and determined worker. But in addition to this, she also had insight and appreciation for the river and its tendencies. Her business savvy cultivated from her years with Thomas, along with the support of her sons and daughter, Elizabeth, contributed to the growth of the business. Susie and

Backman Seafood Company, Sol Legare Road. *Courtesy of Thomas Backman Jr.*

her family would christen the second shrimp trawler the *Backman Elizabeth* in 1973. By the mid-1980s, they had a fleet of six shrimp trawlers: the *Admiral Backman*, *Backman Enterprise*, *Sue Backman*, *Elizabeth*, *Porkey* and the *Backman Brothers*. At one point, Backman Seafood employed over twenty employees.

Susie died in 1990, leaving the business to her sons and daughter. The eldest son, Thomas Jr., became the manager. Backman Seafood continues to operate in its original location, where it has a loyal customer base. Many of Susie and Thomas's descendants still live on James Island.

Alonzo Gilliard

Alonzo Gilliard. *Courtesy Sons of Elijah Masonic Lodge's Archives.*

Alonzo Gilliard was born in 1921. He was married to Suzan Gilliard. Alonzo was the son of Lawrence (1887) and Pricilla Gilliard (1895). During one of my conversations with Alonzo over the years, he said:

> *Frazier, when I was young boy growing up, just about everybody on Sol Legare had a small farm. When the men were not working on their farms, they were fishing, picking oysters, casting for shrimps and crabbing. We lived off the land and the river in those days. I worked on the farm and in the creek with my family until around 1940. Then, as a teenager, I moved to the city of Charleston. I was hired by the Cigar Factory* [American Tobacco Company] *and worked there until I retired.*

Alonzo is a member of Payne RMUE Church on James Island and one of the original fifty-six men who organized the Sons of Elijah Masonic Lodge #457. He is also one of the lodge's past masters. Many of his descendants still live on James Island.

Henry "Bim" Gilliard

Henry "Bim" Gilliard. *Courtesy of Delia Washington.*

Henry "Bim" Gilliard was born in 1900. He was married to Nellie Gilliard (1902). Henry was the son of Stephen (1856) and Delia Gilliard (1867) and the grandson of slave Prince Davis (1837). During an interview with Delia Washington, Henry's daughter, she said:

> *Frazier, my daddy was a hardworking man. He worked as a truck driver on George Nungezer's farm hauling vegetables to the railroad station across from the Windermere Shopping Center, where it would be shipped out of state. He was also a handyman on the farm for many years.*
>
> *He also worked at the Fertilizer Mill in North Charleston sewing bags for years until it closed. To feed his family, he was a fisherman and a farmer. He also learned to make cast nets for shrimp and fish at an early age. He had a wife and six children. He was able to carve a living out of the creek and the land. He was also a boat builder. His love for God, family and community never wavered. He was a member of Payne RMUE Church on Camp Road and a member of ILA lodge on Sol Legare. Prince Davis and Steven's mother were never married.*

Many of Henry Gilliard's descendants still live on James Island.

Clark Plantation

Owners

Julian H. Clark was born in 1924. He was married to Mary Clark (1932). Julian was the son of Julian H. (1882) and Mary Clark (1882) and the grandson of Ephraim (1812) and Susan Clark (1815). Ephraim was the owner of the Clark Plantation during slavery. The Clarks were prominent members of the James Island Presbyterian Church on Fort Johnson Road during the slavery and farming eras. Mary Clark, Julian's wife, became mayor of the Town of James Island after its incorporation was struck down two times by the Supreme Court.

In my conversations with Mayor Mary Clark over the past several years, I could not help but be mesmerized while I listened to her talk about her beloved James Island. She said:

> *I was eleven years old when my family came to Folly Beach in the back of a covered pickup truck. It was 1943, and mother had paid the truck driver to take her and her seven children from a small mountain town in Kentucky to the eastern edge of America. Frazier, in those days there were no interstates. The crowded vehicle drove on Road 25E, winding and turning around mountains.*
>
> *I always had jobs. I sold hot dogs and milk shakes and babysat on Folly Beach to help my mother and father. I graduated near the top of my class from Memminger High School in downtown Charleston in the last graduating class of the all-girls public school. In 1949, when I*

Mayor Mary Clark. *Courtesy of Mayor Mary Clark.*

was seventeen years old, I married Julian Clark, whose family came from a long line of farmers on James Island. I often wondered why he wanted to marry me and not the girls from Ashley Hall, who where always chasing him. I moved to Clark Point, where me and my husband raised turkeys and grew corn. The turkeys were raised on the White House Plantation and the corn was grown on Harborview Road, where the Piggly Wiggly Shopping center stands.

Mrs. Clark reflected on the years that she and her husband farmed the land on James Island. As I listened, it became evident that she knew the history of the island. She mentioned numerous names of African Americans who worked on the Clark farm. She mentioned the name Elder James "Brooks" Williams, an overseer who supervised men such as Arthur Scott, Arthur Ladson, Stephen White and families such as the Washingtons and the Lemons. These are some of the people who either lived or worked on the plantation.

Slaves and Their Descendant

James "Brooks" Williams

James "Brooks" Williams was born in 1896. He was married to Lydia Williams (1898). He was affectionately called "Brooks." His family were farmers, and he was the overseer on the Clark Plantation during the farming and sharecropping eras. Brooks was one of the fifty-six men who helped organize the Sons of Elijah Masonic Lodge #457 on James Island and was appointed its first worshipful master. He was a member of and an elder in the St. James Presbyterian Church until his death. James served in the U.S. Army during World War I.

In one of my last interviews with Harry Eurie prior to his death in 2002, he said:

Son, the Dill family had a commissary on Fort Johnson Road across the road from where the St. James Presbyterian Church is today. The Dills at one time paid the people on the farm with their own paper money that you had to spend at the store. I remember a lot of times my Mama would send me to the store for corn flour and molasses. On many occasions, I would buy a johnnycake, root beer, Pepsi and Royal Crown drink. Each cost three cents. During those days, black people could not buy Coke. One day in 1924, while I was in the store, a black man asked for a Coke. He was a World War I veteran. He was wearing an army uniform. The white man said, "Nigger, you know you all not allow to buy Coke. You better buy this big nigger's drinks or get the hell out of here!" The black man walks out the store with his head bowed down. When I went outside, he sent me back inside to buy him a Royal Crown drink and a johnnycake. I never forgot the sad look on his face and wondered why he said nothing. But Grandpa told me it was best that he say nothing if he didn't want trouble. I learned later James Brooks Williams was the soldier the white man called a nigger. Harry Haley would later operate the store.

Many of James Brooks Williams's descendants still live in the Fort Johnson area of James Island.

Priestly Washington

Priestly Washington. *Courtesy of Pearl McKelvey.*

Priestly Washington was born in 1914. He was married to Essileen Washington. Priestly was the son of Charles "Cesar" (1896) and Lila Washington (1900). Pearl Washington McKelvey, Priestly and Essileen's daughter, said:

Detective, my daddy was what I considered a jack-of-all-trades. He also owned his own farm.

At one time, he worked on the Hinson Plantation during the time when George Nungezer was the manager of the farm and on the Lawton Farm. He also worked for Charleston County government and the Charleston Naval Shipyard in North Charleston.

Detective, he taught his children how to love one another and most of all he taught his children the ways of God. He was a God-fearing man who was very wise and full of the knowledge of God. He was also a humble and funny man. He worked hard to care for his family of seven boys and four girls. Everyone in the neighborhood came to him for help and answers. He loved everyone.

Many of Priestly and Essileen's descendants still live on James Island.

Georgiana Lafayette

Georgiana Lafayette. *Courtesy of Ruth Lafayette.*

Georgiana Lafayette was born in 1898. She was married to Frank Lafayette (1890). Frank was the son of John Lafayette (1845) and a descendant of Frank Lafayette (1800).

Frank worked on the Hinson Plantation during the era when George Nungezer leased the farm, from the 1920s through the 1960s. During an interview with Ruth Lafayette, granddaughter of Georgiana, she said:

Frazier, my grandmother and grandfather, with help from my two aunts, Mae L. Campbell and Louise Williams, raised me. My mother had migrated north to Maryland seeking a better life and job to send money home to help support the family. Although my grandmother did a little farm work, she was a homemaker who did mostly domestic work to help my grandfather earn money to pay the bill.

I attended St. James Parochial School. When school was out, I did some farm work. I attended W. Gresham Meggett High School on James Island and at the age of fourteen, I Joined First Baptist Church on Camp Road. I was the youngest child on the Usher Board during that time. Segregation of the races was enforced, and blacks could not go to the local beaches—Folly Beach or Isles Palms. Blacks had to travel some eighty to one hundred miles to Atlantic Beach to enjoy a swim in the ocean. I was young and was always afraid of crossing the old Cooper River Bridge.

I left Charleston and went to Baltimore, Maryland, to my mother. While there, I finished high school and nursing school. I became a nurse and worked many years in the nursing field. Frazier, I was so proud when I bought my first car—a new 1968 Chevy Nova. I retired in 2003 and came back home to South Carolina in 2004 and bought another home.

Many of Georgina and Frank's descendants still live on James Island.

Mary Lee Lemon Gladden

Mary Lee Lemon Gladden.
Courtesy of Ruth Lafayette.

Mary Lee Lemon Gladden was born in 1906. She was married to Joe Gladden (1906). Mary Lee was the daughter of George (1878) and Lena Lemon (1882) and the granddaughter of slaves Geoffrey (1845) and Lena Washington (1882).

Mary Lee was affectionately called "Sister" by the people in the community. Although she was born and raised in the Fort Johnson area, after her marriage to Joe, they moved to the Dill Plantation and became sharecroppers and eventually farmers during the time when Fuller King was manager of the Dill Plantation. I recall when Joe Gladden died in 1945; I walked behind the funeral procession on Grimball Road, which was dirt at the time. The funeral was handled by Fielding Funeral Home. During this time, the hearse that they used resembled a paddy wagon once used by the police department years ago. Joe was buried at the cemetery called Devil's Nest on the Dill Plantation, adjacent to the Carolina Skyways Airport and the Grimball Plantation property line near the Stono River.

Cyrus Jr. and Diana Frazier

Cyrus Frazier Jr. was born in 1909. He was married to Diana McKelvey Frazier (1915). Cyrus was the grandson of slaves Cyrus Sr. (1852) and Rosa

Above, left: Cyrus Frazier Jr. *Family photographs.*

Above, right: Diana McKelvey Frazier. *Family photographs.*

Frazier (1852). They were farmers on the Grimball Plantation. Diana was the daughter of Esow (1890) and Elizabeth McKelvey (1890) and the granddaughter of slaves Rollie (1842) and Betty McKelvey (1860). They were farmers on the Hinson/Mikell Plantation.

Cyrus worked for the *News & Courier* in Charleston and retired after some twenty years. He was also a farmer. He was a member of and an elder in the St. James Presbyterian Church on James Island and one of the original fifty-six men who helped organized the Sons of Elijah Lodge #457 on James Island. Many of Cyrus and Diana's descendants still live in the Fort Johnson area of James Island.

Harry and Mary Haley

Harry Haley was born in 1897. He was married to Mary Haley (1899). Harry Haley was a farmer. Mary Haley operated the wooden grocery store on the first floor of their house at the corner of Fort Johnson and

Left: Harry and Mary Haley standing on the step of their house at the corner of Fort Johnson and Secessionville Roads. *Courtesy of Gladys Haley.*

Above: Mary Haley. *Courtesy of Gladys Haley.*

Secessionville Roads. It was across the road from the St. James Presbyterian Church and the St. James Parochial School during the farming era. Mrs. Haley was especially proud of the fact that she never sold alcohol beverages in the thirty-five years of the store's history.

During the slavery and sharecropping eras, the land farmed by Mr. Haley was owned by Joseph T. Dill of the Dill Plantation. The Haleys were members of the James Island Presbyterian Church on Fort Johnson Road. In the early 1940s, while attending the St. James Parochial School, I recall that students whose parents could afford to give them extra money besides the ten cents for the school lunch would go across the road to buy candies and cookies at the store.

Woodrow Singelton Sr.

Woodrow Singelton Sr. was the first African American hired as a police officer from James Island by the Charleston City Police Department. He was assigned to the traffic division until he retired in 1985.

Woodrow Sr. is married to the former Althea Richardson. They have two sons, Woodrow Jr. (deceased) and Lerone, and two daughters, Euconfra

and Tammy Singelton. Woodrow Sr. was the son of Laura Singelton Todd (1922) and Andrew "Apple" Wilder (1915). Althea was the daughter of John Sr. (1910) and Edna "Mattie" Richardson (1914). Many of Woodrow's family and relatives still live on James Island.

Eugene Frazier Sr.

I was the first African American hired as a police officer from James Island by the Charleston County Police Sheriff's Office. I rose through the ranks to become a lieutenant. During my career, I worked as a detective sergeant in the Homicide Division for fourteen years. I retired as a lieutenant after twenty-five years of service. I joined the U.S. Marshal Court Security Service and worked at the Broad and Meeting Street Office for eight years. I am the son of Sandy (1908) and Viola Smalls Frazier (1908). Many of my family and relatives still live on James Island.

Silas B. Welch

Silas B. Welch was born in 1916 and died in 2002. He was married to Virginia R. Welch. Silas was the son of Silas S. Welch Sr. (1882–1950) and Naomi Bailey Welch (1893–1973). Silas and Virginia lived on James Island until their deaths.

Top: Woodrow Singelton Sr. *Courtesy of Edna "Mattie" Richardson.*

Middle: Eugene Frazier Sr. *Courtesy of Eugene Frazier Sr.*

Bottom: Chief Silas B. Welch. *Courtesy Charleston County Library.*

During the 1960s, South Carolina was still enforcing segregation of the races, and there were no blacks on the Charleston County Police Force. The County Police Department's headquarters was moved from its location in Charleston on Huston Street to Pinehaven Drive in North Charleston. Prior to the move, Chief Welch hired its first two black police officers, James L. Mikell and George H. Gathers.

When I was hired, Chief Welch called me into his office and said:

> *Frazier, after looking at your resume, I see that you served six years in the army and was discharged as a sergeant. You have to use that experience and be thick skinned. I am going to be frank with you. There are whites that don't want to take orders from a black police officer, and some politicians are against hiring blacks. Just use your military experience and prove them wrong. Make me and your race proud.*

I have always said from the beginning of my career that Chief Welch was a good and decent man.

During the 1960s, Dr. Martin Luther King Jr. was appearing all over the country speaking out against the injustices suffered by African Americans in the United States. In 1967, Dr. King was invited to speak at a meeting at the Charleston County Hall by then president of the Charleston Chapter of the NAACP, J. Arthur Brown, who made the request through the county council for protection for Dr. King's visit.

Chief Welch summoned the late detectives J.L. Mikel and George H. Gathers and me into his office. I was a patrolman at the time. The chief

Far left: Detective James L. Mikel. *Family picture.*

Left: Detective George H. Gathers. *Family picture.*

told us that we were to meet Dr. King at the Municipal Airport and escort him to Charleston County Hall, where we would stay with him until he finished his business in Charleston. We were then to return him to the airport and ensure that he got safely on the plane. He also cautioned us that if any harm came to Dr. King while he was in Charleston, he would personally hold the three of us responsible. He added that we would be looking for a job because we would be terminated. We assured the chief that Dr. King would be protected while we guarded him and that we were prepared. It is now a sad and tragic part of history that this great leader was assassinated one year later, in April 1968, in Memphis, Tennessee. His legacy will be forever cherished. His accomplishments in the area of civil rights paved the way for all African Americans. We will be forever indebted to him.

Churches

The James Island Presbyterian Church on Fort Johnson Road is often referred to as the "white" Presbyterian church to distinguish it from the Presbyterian church on Secessionville Road, whose members are 98 percent black.

The original church's structure was destroyed by a fire that was accidentally set by a Confederate soldier in a field behind the church in 1865. Between 1833 and 1845, according to minutes obtained from the church's archives, there were 153 slaves, 1 freed slave and 33 white members attending the church. During a conversation with my cousin, Frank Deleston (1875), he said, "Son, my papa said some of the slaves that tend [attended] the white church with him was Joseph Deleston [1838]; your great-grandpa, Ben "Benjamin" Frazier [1828]; Freeman Cromwell [1841]; and Truman Cromwell [1854]."

According to the church's achieves, after the church was destroyed by fire, the white members held worship services at the home of Mr. Ephraim Clark, owner of the Clark Plantation. With no place to worship, the former slaves held worship services under an oak tree at the corner of Fort Johnson and Secessionville Roads. In 1866, Reverend Henry H. Hunter came from the north to teach the newly freed slaves to read and write. By 1868, he had successfully built the first St. James Presbyterian Church at the corner of Fort Johnson and Secessionville Roads for the sum of $800. He taught classes in the church during the week and held worship services on Sunday. He died in 1893.

James Island Presbyterian Church on James Island. *Family photograph.*

Reverend Marion A. Sanders was born in 1888. He was married to Ona Belle Sanders (1898). In 1923, Reverend Marion A. Sanders accepted the call to pastor at the St. James Presbyterian Church. He came from Charlotte, North Carolina, to James Island. He saw the need for and immediately reopened the Mission School. Classes were held in the church during the week.

In 1924, with the blessing of the church elders, he bought a three-room board house and had it rolled across the road onto the church's property. He then renamed the Mission School the St. James Parochial School. Reverend Sanders and Mrs. Sanders taught at the school from 1923 until their retirement in 1961.

My aunt, Ethel F. Campbell, was born in 1917. Ethel was among the students in the first class at St. James Parochial School in 1924. During this time, Reverend Marion A. Sanders was the headmaster, and his wife, Ona Belle Sanders, was the administrator for the school.

Ethel was the first female majorette selected in 1930 by Mrs. Ona Belle Sanders for the now-famous May Day Festival on James Island. This celebration is now carried out in many of the Sea Island areas annually. Aunt Ethel is a member of St. James Presbyterian Church. She has also held the positions of elder and division leader in the church.

During one of several interviews held with her over the years, she said:

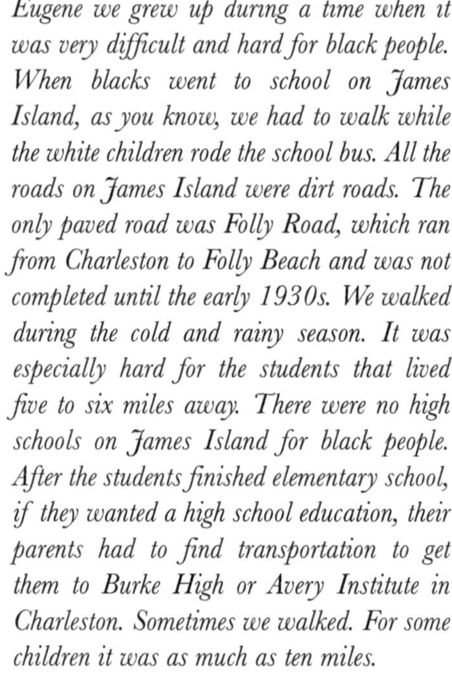

Eugene we grew up during a time when it was very difficult and hard for black people. When blacks went to school on James Island, as you know, we had to walk while the white children rode the school bus. All the roads on James Island were dirt roads. The only paved road was Folly Road, which ran from Charleston to Folly Beach and was not completed until the early 1930s. We walked during the cold and rainy season. It was especially hard for the students that lived five to six miles away. There were no high schools on James Island for black people. After the students finished elementary school, if they wanted a high school education, their parents had to find transportation to get them to Burke High or Avery Institute in Charleston. Sometimes we walked. For some children it was as much as ten miles.

Many of Ethel and Herbert's family still live on James Island.

The Parochial School was located at the corner of Fort Johnson and Secessionville Roads on the property where the St. James Presbyterian Church stands today. The memorial monument is also located on the church's property and is dedicated to the memory of Reverend H.H. Hunter, Reverend Marion Sanders, Mrs. Ona Belle Sanders and the teachers of the St. James Parochial

Top: Reverend Marion A. Sanders. *Courtesy of Ruth Lafayette.*

Middle: Ona Belle Sanders. *Courtesy of Ruth Lafayette.*

Bottom: Ethel F. Campbell. *Family photograph.*

From left to right: Maggie Belle Sanders McFadden; my sister, Ursalee Frazier; and Levola Whaley at the former site of the St. James Parochial School. This picture was taken during the dedication service of the monument honoring the teachers and the Reverend Marion A. and Ona Belle Sanders. *Family photograph.*

The St. James Parochial School monument.

St. James Presbyterian Church (present). *Family photograph.*

Above, left: Reverend Cornelius Campbell. *Courtesy of Mrs. Hattie Campbell.*

Above, right: Reverend Bernard J. Gadsden Sr., pastor, First Baptist Church. *Courtesy of Reverend Bernard J. Gadsden Sr.*

School. The monument was erected by some of the former students of the St. James Parochial School and its president, Eugene Frazier, in 2003.

The beautiful St. James Presbyterian Church standing today was built in 1977 under the pastoral leadership and vision of Reverend Cornelius L. Campbell, who accepted the call to pastor the church in 1970. Reverend Campbell served faithfully until his untimely death in 1993.

First Baptist Church

The First Baptist Church, 2010.

After slavery, a wooden house owned by the Fergerson family was used as a church. The house was located at the corner of Camp and Dills Bluff Road. Many ministers served at the church after slavery and during the farming era. Reverend Bernard J. Gadsden Sr., the church's current pastor, was installed in 1987. Under his leadership, this beautiful church was built at the corner of Dill Bluff and Camp Roads, completed in 2009.

RMUE Church

After slavery, Elizabeth Seabrook, owner of the Seabrook Plantation, gave the property on Camp Road to her overseer, Prince "Pappy" White (1830), and the former slaves who lived on the plantation. There, the first Payne RMUE Church was built, and its first pastor was Reverend Prince "Pappy" White (1830). Numerous preachers have served as pastors at the church since its founding. Some of these pastors were Reverend Bernard Brown, Reverend Joseph U. Grant, Reverend James Blake, Reverend Arthur Blunt, Reverend John H. Moore, Reverend Wesmore White, Reverend Hercules Champagne and the Reverend Joseph Powell.

Above, left: Reverend Thomas Junious, pastor, Payne RMUE Church. *Courtesy of Reverend Thomas Junious.*

Above, right: The Payne RMUE Church on Camp Road, James Island, as it is today. *Courtesy of Eugene Frazier.*

Elder Thomas Junious was appointed as pastor of Payne RMUE Church in November 2006. According to members, it was a blessing to see this high-spirited servant of God arrive. It was a boost to their congregation, and his appointment as pastor illustrates the phrase, "The young is strong and the old know the way." They believe that he is truly anointed by God and demonstrates his love for all people, just as our Lord and Savior has commanded us to do. He urges his congregation to exert a disciplined commitment to serving God. He is described as courageous, soul stirring, God-fearing, energetic and bubbly, with the goal of taking Payne Church to greater heights. Elder Junious resides in Summerton, South Carolina, and commutes to Charleston several times weekly with his beautiful wife, first lady Ruth Junious, and their two daughters, Faith and Hope. His congregation believes that their support of Payne Church is commendable and illustrates their dedication to the building up of God's Kingdom.

Tribute to Pioneers and Trailblazers

This chapter is a special tribute to and recognition of the men in Charleston County who were among the first black men to be hired at various organizations. They helped to integrate the different organizations but had to suffer pain, indignity and frustration in order to gain that distinction. They helped to pave the way for future African Americans to become gainfully employed in those organizations. It is my belief that these pioneers deserve a special place in history for their courage and dignity in the face of numerous hardships and oppression.

Eight African American men were hired as policemen in the city of Charleston in 1950. The black officers were not allowed to ride in or to drive patrol cars, as segregation was strictly enforced. They were also not allowed to arrest white people, and if a black officer witnessed a crime being committed by a white person, he could only hold the suspect until a white officer arrived in a patrol car to take the suspect to jail. They were assigned to walk beats in predominantly black areas.

This group of African American officers was hired during Mayor Palmer Gilliard's and Chief William Kelly's administrations. All of these pioneers are now deceased. Many blacks still refer to the deceased as "traveling on a level of time to that undiscovered country, from who born no traveler returns to receive their final reward that only God can give."

Josie Wong and Cambridge Jenkins were the first two African Americans hired as SLED agents in South Carolina in 1962. They were appointed by then governor Ernest "Fritz" Hollings from Charleston while they were

The first group of African Americans hired by the Charleston Police Department. *From left to right*: James L. Mikel, Walter Burke, Christopher B. Ward, Ernest Deveaux, Monte Heighten, George Gathers, Cambridge Jenkins and Bennie Taylor. *Courtesy of Fred Stroble.*

employed by the Charleston City Police Department. Four years later, they returned to Charleston. Josie Wong would rejoin the city police department as a detective, and Cambridge Jenkins would be appointed the first black deputy United States marshal from South Carolina.

Fred Stroble was hired as a city police officer in 1962. He was one of the first two blacks appointed to the Motor Cycle Squad. He rose to the rank of detective and became the first black deputy sheriff hired in Charleston County. In 1972, he became the second black deputy U.S. marshal from Charleston and the third from South Carolina. Following his retirement from the marshal service, he began another career as a court security officer (CSO) for the Federal District Court in Charleston, located at the corner of Broad and Meeting Streets. Fred still lives in the metropolitan area. Many of his children and relatives still live in Charleston.

Alonzo Haynes, thirty-third degree mason, was the first African American from Charleston, South Carolina, to be elected most worshipful grand master of the Most Worshipful Prince Hall Grand Lodge of Free and Accepted Masons, Jurisdictional of South Carolina. The Masonic Grand Temple is located at 2324 Gervais Street in Columbia, South Carolina.

Clockwise, from top left: Josie Wong. *Courtesy of Darryl Wong*; Cambridge Jenkins. *Courtesy of Avery Institute*; Fred Stroble. *Courtesy of Fred Stroble*; Alonzo Haynes. *Courtesy of Alonzo Haynes.*

Lonnie Hamilton III. *Courtesy of Lonnie Hamilton III.*

Between March 2, and June 30, 1784, African Lodge No. 1 applied to the Grand Lodge of England for a charter. On September 29, 1784, a charter was granted for African Lodge #459. This order was executed by the authority of the Duke of Cumberland, the grand master of the Mother Grand Lodge in England. Prince Hall was elected its first Worshipful Grand Master Lodge.

Lonnie Hamilton III was an educator who ran for a seat on the Charleston County Council in 1970. The young educator went on to win the election with his pledge to represent all people, regardless of race. His win made him the first African American to hold that office. He would win reelection continually from 1970 to 1990, some twenty years. During his tenure, he served twice as chairman and once as vice-chairman while on the county council.

Tribute to Members of the Armed Forces

This chapter is a special tribute to the men and women from James Island who unselfishly served their country in the armed forces during times of peace, as well as during World War I, World War II, the Korean War, the Vietnam War, the Gulf and Iraq Wars and Operation Desert Storm.

Some of them gave the ultimate sacrifice—their lives—in order to make this country safer for all of us. I join the family members of these men and women and the citizens of James Island to give thanks and appreciation to all of these exceptional men and women, including those who are not listed.

Clockwise from top left:

Josiah Brown, U.S. Army, World War II. He received a Purple Heart/Bronze Medal. *Courtesy of Dorothy Brown Thomas.*

Henry "Sleepy" Burden, U.S. Navy, World War II. *Courtesy of Nathaniel Frazier.*

James Richardson, U.S. Army, World War I. He received a letter from President Richard Nixon honoring him. *Courtesy of Edna M. Richardson.*

Clockwise from top left:

Arthur Lee Chisolm, U.S. Marine Corp. He was killed in Vietnam in 1968. *Courtesy of Vivian Chisolm.*

Eugene Frazier Jr., chief E-7, U.S. Navy, retired. *Family photograph.*

Theodore Richardson, U.S. Army. He was killed in Vietnam 1965. *Courtesy of Edna Richardson.*

Clockwise from top left:

Woodrow Singelton Jr., master sergeant E-8, U.S Army, Iraq War, deceased—service related. *Courtesy of Aletha Singleton.*

George Washington, chief E-7, U.S. Navy, retired. *Courtesy of George Washington.*

James "Fed" Frazier, U.S. Army, World War II. *Courtesy of Elouise Frazier.*

Clockwise from top left:

Edward Green, sergeant E-5, U.S. Army, Vietnam War. *Courtesy of Edward Green.*

Francis Bolds, chief E-8, U.S. Navy, retired, World War II, Vietnam War. *Courtesy of Francis Bolds.*

Lloyd Young, specialist fourth class, U.S. Army, Vietnam War. *Courtesy of Lloyd Young.*

Clockwise from top left:

Abraham Brown, first sergeant E-9, U.S. Army, Vietnam War. *Courtesy of Abraham Brown.*

Daniel Brown, corporal E-4, U.S. Army, Vietnam War. *Courtesy of Daniel Brown.*

Wilburn Gilliard, sergeant E-5, U. S. Army, Vietnam War. *Courtesy of Wilburn Gilliard.*

Clockwise from top left:

Henry Richardson, sergeant E-5, U.S. Army. He was given the Purple Heart for his service in the Vietnam War. *Courtesy Henry Richardson.*

Isaac Gathers, sergeant E-7, U.S. Army, retired. *Courtesy of Isaac Gathers.*

Charles Richard Mack, master sergeant E-9, U.S. Army, retired, Korean War, Vietnam War. *Courtesy of Charles R. Mack.*

Clockwise from top left:

Ronald Middleton, sergeant E-5, U.S. Army, Vietnam War. He received three Purple Hearts. *Courtesy of Ronald Middleton.*

James "Mickey" Middleton, E-4, U.S. Navy. He served during the Vietnam era. *Courtesy of James Middleton.*

Sipio Williams, gunnery sergeant, U.S. Marine Corps. He was killed in Beirut in 1980. *Courtesy of Janis Williams.*

Clockwise from top left:

Keith Bright, master sergeant E-8, U.S. Air Force, retired, Iraq. *Courtesy of Keith Bright.*

Edward McKelvey Sr., specialist fourth class, U.S. Army. *Courtesy of Edward McKelvey.*

Jack Walker, corporal E-4, U.S. Army. *Courtesy of Ann W. Rivers.*

Clockwise from top left:

Joseph Deleston Jr., corporal E-4, U.S. Army. *Courtesy of Marie Deleston.*

James Frazier, U.S. Air Force, Vietnam War. *Courtesy Eugene Frazier.*

William Roper, master sergeant E-8, U.S. Air Force, retired. *Courtesy of William Roper.*

Clockwise from top left:

Alfred "Bob" Gourdine, corporal E4, U.S. Army. *Courtesy of Alfred Gourdine.*

Eugene Frazier, sergeant E-6, U.S. Army, Korean War. *Family photograph.*

James Walker, corporal E-4, U.S. Army, Vietnam War. *Courtesy of James Walker.*

Clockwise from top left:

Benjamin Chisolm, sergeant E-6, U.S. Army, Vietnam War. *Courtesy of Adrian C. Cox.*

Wayne Moore, gunnery sergeant, U.S. Marine Corps. *Courtesy of Keith Bright.*

Avery Wilder, sergeant E-5, U.S. Army. He was killed in Vietnam. *Family photograph.*

Clockwise from top left:

Thomas Johnson, master chief, U.S. Navy, retired, Vietnam War. *Courtesy of Thomas Johnson.*

Alexander Chisolm, lance corporal, U.S. Marine Corps. He was killed in Vietnam in 1966. *Family photograph.*

Joe Richardson Jr., corporal E-4, U.S. Army. *Family photograph.*

Clockwise from top left:

Eric Johnson, lieutenant commander 0-4, U.S. Navy. *Courtesy of Thomas Johnson.*

Leroy Deleston, specialist third class, U.S. Army. *Courtesy of Elaine William.*

Tyrone Johnson, sergeant major E-9, U.S. Army. *Courtesy of Thomas Johnson.*

Clockwise from top left:

Franklin Moultrie, corporal E-4, U.S. Marine Corps. *Courtesy of Nellie Clark.*

Nathaniel Frazier, sergeant E-7, U.S. Army, retired. *Courtesy of Elouise Frazier.*

Rubin Fergerson, sergeant E-7, U.S. Army, retired, Vietnam War. *Courtesy Rosa Lee Fergerson.*

Clockwise from top left:

Virgil Smalls, chief E-7, U.S. Navy, Vietnam War, Gulf War. *Courtesy of Rita Smalls.*

Leroy Brown Prioleau, corporal E-4, U.S. Army. *Family photograph.*

Ronald Cromwell, sergeant E-5, U.S. Marine Corps, Vietnam War. *Courtesy of Ronald Cromwell.*

Clockwise from top left:

Kenneth Deleston, E-4, U.S. Air Force. *Courtesy of Kenneth Deleston.*

Rubin "Trey" Fergerson, warrant officer, U.S. Army, Iraq War, active duty. *Courtesy of Rosa Lee Fergerson.*

Oswald "Bucky" Moore, private first class E-3, U.S. Army. *Courtesy of Adrian Chisolm Cox.*

Clockwise from top left:

Benjamin "Benny" Chisolm, U.S. Navy, World War II. *Courtesy Francis E. Frazier.*

George Prioleau Jr., sergeant E-7, U.S. Army National Guard. *Courtesy of George Prioleau.*

Arthur Moultrie Drayton. *Family photograph.*

Clockwise from top left:

Prince Brown, E-3, U.S. Army, Vietnam War. *Courtesy of Prince White.*

Herbert "Bubba" Cromwell Jr., U.S. Army, Vietnam War. *Courtesy of Rosalee Fergerson.*

George Lafayette, sergeant E-5, U.S. Army, World War II. *Courtesy Genevieve Lafayette.*

Clockwise from top left:

Hezekiah Richardson, corporal E-4, U.S. Army, Korean War. *Courtesy of Mary Richardson*.

Charles H. Whaley Jr., U.S. Air Force. *Courtesy of Catharine Whaley Singelton*.

George L. Whaley, U.S. Marine Corps, Vietnam War. *Courtesy Catherine W. Singelton*.

Clockwise from top left:

Josiah Singelton, sergeant E-5, U.S. Army, World War II. *Courtesy Catherine W. Singelton.*

Eddie Singelton, U.S. Marine Corps. *Courtesy of Ethelyn Singelton.*

Richard Brown, U.S. Air Force. *Courtesy Ethelyn Singelton.*

Clockwise from top left:

Willie Singelton, U.S. Army. *Courtesy of Ruth Ann Singleton.*

Kevin T. Young, chief warrant officer, U.S. Army. *Courtesy of Ruth Ann Singleton.*

Johnny Davis, master sergeant E-9, U.S. Air Force. *Courtesy of Lucile Jordon.*

Clockwise from top left:

Gordon Brown Sr., specialist fourth class, U.S. Army. *Courtesy of McKeever Brown Jr.*

McKeever Brown Jr., technical sergeant, U.S. Air Force, retired. *Courtesy of McKeever Brown Jr.*

Joe Brown, private first class E-3, U.S. Army. *Courtesy of Joe Brown.*

Clockwise from top left:

Tony Richardson, U.S. Air Force. *Courtesy of John Richardson.*

Carlton "CJ" Washington, petty officer second class, U.S. Navy. *Courtesy Estel Washington.*

Hasco Seymour, technical sergeant, U.S. Air Force. *Courtesy of Hasco Seymour.*

Clockwise from top left:

Bernard Hamilton, corporal E4, U.S. Army. *Courtesy of Wilhelmina Hamilton.*

Rodney Cromwell, U.S. Army. *Courtesy of Ruby Cromwell.*

George Cromwell, U.S. Army. *Courtesy of Ruby Cromwell.*

Clockwise from top left:

Reginald Wright, sergeant, U.S. Army. *Courtesy of Reginald Wright.*

Ceser Jenkins, chief master sergeant E-9, U.S. Army, retired. *Courtesy of Cesar Jenkins.*

Elias Urie, U.S. Marine Corps. *Courtesy of Janet Urie White.*

Clockwise from top left:

Keith Urie , U.S. Navy. *Courtesy of Janet Urie White.*

Glenn Urie, U.S. Army. *Courtesy of Janet Urie White.*

Stacy Williams, sergeant E-5, U.S. Army, Criminal Investigation Command. *Courtesy of Stacey Williams.*

Clockwise from top left:

Cornelius Richardson, second lieutenant, U.S. Army, World War II, Korean War. *Courtesy of Cornelius Richardson.*

Ronald Richardson, U.S. Air Force. *Courtesy of Alonzo Richardson.*

Clayton Cromwell, sergeant E-5, U.S. Army. *Family photograph.*

Clockwise from top left:

Arcell M. Richardson, U.S. Navy. *Courtesy of Bell Whaley.*

Cicero Whaley, U.S. Navy. *Courtesy of Bell Whaley.*

Louis Gourdine, corporal E 4, U.S. Army. *Courtesy of Louis Gourdine.*

Clockwise from top left:

Marion Matthews, sergeant E-5, U.S. Army. *Courtesy of Marion Matthews.*

Samuel Rufus Bright, sergeant first class E-7, U.S. Army. *Courtesy of Samuel Bright.*

Mark Whaley, sergeant first class E-7, U.S. Army. *Courtesy of Mark Whaley.*

Clockwise from top left:

Byron Minter, chief E-7, U.S. Navy, retired. *Family photograph.*

Albertha Deleston Hamilton, U.S. Army, Women's Army Corps (WAC), Korean War. *Courtesy of Lillian Whaley.*

Euconfra Singelton, sergeant E-5, U.S. Army. *Courtesy Althea Singelton.*

Clockwise from top left:

Elise Cromwell, corporal E-4, U.S. Army. *Courtesy Elise Cromwell.*

Meldina Washington, U.S. Army. *Courtesy of Ruthann Singelton.*

Gwendolyn Washington, sergeant E-6, U.S. Army, Gulf War. *Courtesy of Nellie Clark.*

Clockwise from top left:

Pamela Backman Brown, sergeant E-5, U.S. Army, Gulf War. *Courtesy of Pamela C. Brown.*

Gearline Richardson Cross, technical sergeant, U.S. Air Force. *Courtesy John Richardson.*

Kate S. Urie, command master sergeant E-9, U.S. Air Force. *Courtesy of Janet S. Urie.*

Clockwise from top left:

Brenda Middleton, captain, U.S. Army. *Courtesy of Carrie Middleton.*

Stacia Williams, sergeant E-6, U.S. Air Force. *Courtesy of Margret Grippon.*

Carla Middleton, sergeant E5, U.S. Army. *Courtesy of Carrie Middleton.*

Fatima V. Rivers, sergeant E5, U.S. Army. *Courtesy of Ann Rivers.*

Standing in the second row, fourth from the left, is Private Mary L. Lafayette from Sol Legare, James Island. Ms. Lafayette was among the first group of African American women to serve in the Women's Army Corps (WAC) during World War II from South Carolina. This picture is of Company D, First Battalion, at the training center in Fort Lee, Virginia. *Courtesy of Genevese Lafayette.*

Special Tribute to Shawn Riley, My Nephew

Our family is not complete without you. Your presence is missed. God bless you always.

In Conclusion

The slaves, starting with the first generation brought to James Island from the west coast of Africa and other parts of the world, were determined to make a better life for themselves. Many of the slaves went north by way of the Underground Railroad during slavery. During the sharecropping and farming eras, many blacks migrated north to escape the degradation and hardship of life on the farms. However, the majority of the descendants of slaves who remained on the plantations continued to labor tirelessly over the years. They were determined to make a better life for themselves and their descendants.

James Island, during this period, was like a wilderness with farmland and woods. Over the years, the slaves, along with their owners, cleared the land to make room for the seventeen plantations. From the beginning, they planted and harvested rice and cotton and raised cattle, cows, horses, mules and chickens on these plantations. Now, after more than two hundred years, James Island is a bristling community of which native African Americans are proud to be a part. These African Americans have helped this island develop into a modern town and a flourishing urban area by their sheer determination and tenacity.

About the Author

Eugene Frazier Sr. is married to the former Frances E. Prioleau. They have one son, Eugene Jr.; two daughters, Geraldine and Angela; one daughter-in-law, Lee; one son-in-law, Byron; six grandchildren, Eugene III, Gregory, Jamal, Leah, Jehrica and Brian; and one great-granddaughter, Kaylee. Eugene is a retired police lieutenant who served twenty-five years with the Charleston County Sheriff's Office and eight years with the U.S. Marshal Service. He served six years in the United States Army and was honorably discharged as a sergeant E-6. He is a member of the St. James Presbyterian Church on James Island. He is a former Sunday school teacher, chairman of the Men's Council and a former member of the council's trustee board and sits on the board of directors for the Friends of McLeod. He is also a member of the organization to preserve and protect African American cemeteries on James Island. He is a thirty-second degree Mason and the present worshipful master of the Sons of Elijah Masonic Lodge #457. He is a member of the Charleston County Constituent School Board #3 on James Island and the author of two previous books: *From Segregation to Integration: The Making of a Black Policeman* and *James Island: Stories from Slave Descendants.*

www.ingramcontent.com/pod-product-compliance
Lightning Source LLC
Chambersburg PA
CBHW041752010726
47507CB00009B/368

* 9 7 8 1 5 9 6 2 9 9 7 6 4 *